ABC's of Library Promotion

Third Edition

by

STEVE SHERMAN

The Scarecrow Press, Inc.
Metuchen, N.J., & London
1992

British Library Cataloguing-in-Publication data available

Library of Congress Cataloging-in-Publication Data

Sherman, Steve, 1938–
    ABC's of library promotion / by Steve Sherman. — 3rd ed.
        p.   cm.
    Includes bibliographical references and index.
    ISBN 0-8108-2569-4 (alk. paper)
    1. Public relations—Libraries.   I. Title.
Z716.3.S45   1992
021.7—dc20   92-23330

Contents

PART TWO

PART THREE

APPENDIXES

Preface to the Third Edition

During the last decade significant changes occurred that now affect the future operation of libraries. Economically, socially, and culturally, our country twisted and turned to new directions, influencing the day-to-day function of libraries everywhere. We shifted from a creditor to a debtor nation for the first time in seventy years. Today our international trade deficit and federal budget deficit interplay against the vitality and inventiveness of our better years. The gap between the rich and poor has enlarged at an alarming rate, and homelessness has become a national disgrace (in fact, for a time the homeless used some libraries for day shelters). At the same time, illiteracy—an intellectual virus that eats at the core of libraries—emerged from our national closet of secrets.

The last decade resulted in the decrease of federal and state funds allocated to libraries and the arts under the problematical, sometimes deceptive, prophecy that private enterprise would tighten the slack and come to the rescue. Nothing of the sort happened to the extent that was professed, largely because Americans progress in reaction to crisis, and libraries seldom are viewed by nonlibrarians as in a state of crisis. Instead, user fees increased, and the concept that libraries were shared sources of information and entertainment for everyone, including the poor, deteriorated.

In view of all this, librarians are challenged more than ever. They must tell their tale of what libraries are all about, how they contribute to the village and nation, and what their very existence means to the vitality of an informed, questioning, people-ruling democracy.

Five new chapters have been added to this edition, and many sections and references have been updated. One of the chapters—"Campaigning for Funds"—speaks to an increasingly important focus for the next decade. Librarians must address the need to generate budget financing from private and municipal sectors. With emphasis on the public relations aspect, this chapter follows the step-by-step example of how the Keene (N.H.) Public Library conducted its successful campaign, not for a new building or an addition but for books, tapes, and other lending materials.

This book is intended to help librarians promote their services, materials, and contributions. In turn, this helps justify their purchases and storage of resources, maintain and expand their budgets, engender patron good will and support, and underscore the value of their libraries to the community they serve.

Steve Sherman
Hancock, New Hampshire

PART ONE

1 The Necessity of Public Relations

The reputation for power and influence that the field of public relations enjoys is undeniable. Part of the reputation stems from public relations agencies themselves acting as a mechanism for self-propulsion. On the other hand, much of the reputation springs from actually seeing once-unknown people with less-than-sterling talents transformed into Professional Personalities. It happens all the time, and television is the prime source of confirmation. Clever agencies can, often for a sum of money more impressive than a client's craft, transform performers or artists or politicians into household words with suddenly flaring national and international reputations. This power encompasses not only people and things but ideas as well.

The power of directing our attention, choices, likes and dislikes, prejudices, and opinions is clear. We vote for a politician in a measure larger than we realize because of good behind-the-scenes press relations. We buy a product in large measure because of skillful advertising. We attend a performance in large measure because of effective public relations. The politicians, the products, and the performances are known to us so that they may fulfill their purposes and we may use them in the broadest, most beneficent sense.

The key is to realize that they were not always known. They became known.

What Public Relations Is Not

Often the connotation of public relations instills a knee-jerk cynicism. Unfortunately, such an automatic reaction may dissuade librarians from paying attention to what public relations may do for them appropriately and honorably. Using the methods and procedures of advertising need not be

3

dishonest, tricky, shady, or untruthful. Nor need they lower the prestige or self-respect of librarians.

Public relations for libraries need not be the means of turning a library into a circus with bookshelves. Librarians don't need to hawk their wares like sideshow barkers or wear purple striped shirts and dresses under chartreuse beanie caps with plastic propellers to make their point. This may be PR for used-car dealers and county-fair callers. It isn't and shouldn't be public relations for librarians.

What Public Relations Is

The names for public relations run the gamut from PR and community relations to public affairs and customer service. In the end, it distills to the historic term of public relations—the art and technique of relating to the public. Letting the populace know your message. Telling people at large what you have to offer. Displaying your wares for open view.

Public relations in effect fulfills the potential of your services and products. It helps make libraries dynamic centers of informational and recreational needs rather than buildings where librarians get jobs. It makes them living structures of humanity's attempt at the divine rather than grey halls of evidence past. It enlivens libraries to become aggressive wheels in the knowledge whirl of the contemporary scene rather than plodding stables of a quickly bored society.

Public relations also acknowledges the need to give the public its just due. Libraries are for serving the public, not librarians. The people cannot know how a library may fully serve them if they do not know this potential. They certainly should know, since every kind of library is financed by the people it is designed to serve. Unless the people know and are graciously invited to use the materials, they will not touch the books, periodicals, films, microfiche, ultramicrofiche, maps, optical scanners, computers, video tapes, phonorecords, film-strips, union catalogs, story hours, art prints, and all the rest waiting especially for them.

In the last analysis, good public relations for libraries is directed to an enriched quality of service. Public relations is the harvest, not the seed. A library enjoys good relations with its public as a result of excellent service and use of its materials, not as a result of public relations per se. Fine service means an attention to what urges the public to enter the premises and enjoy the visit. If welcoming smiles and orderly shelves urge one segment of the public to enjoy your library, then such service is appropriate and effective. Call this public relations. As far as libraries are concerned, effectively promoting the use of libraries *is* good service. And good service is good public relations.

Rule One

Love the place. Without loving your library, your work, your field, then all the public relations tricks of the trade in the world will not persuade too many people for long that you have what they want. What your library is, what you are, and how you see yourself in your field will be the core of any successful public relations program.

So like your job and let it show. Improve the place. Brighten the corners with flowers. Make the space inviting to enter and use. Know your library so well and find it so attractive that you'll want to share it as much as possible.

Rule Two

Tell people about your library. That's good service, because then they'll think of it, use it, tell others about the profitable experience they had there. They can't use what they don't know. If the library doesn't exist for them, then they won't exist for the library. If they know only what they think a library always was and therefore always will be, they'll use only a fraction of what you know it now offers.

An effortless mistake is to feel that library services and materials are important in themselves and therefore it is unnecessary to publicize them. Inherent value, like virtue, will win out. The good will triumph. Truth will reign.

So we think.

People not only must be told about what a library has to offer, but they like to be told. Libraries change. They're alive.

They grow bigger, better, have more special services to offer. And people change. They find new needs in themselves, seek new answers, new activities, new people, new places. No matter in how small a way, a service that helps fulfill them is an extraordinary blessing. They're most appreciative.

The promotion of library services, then, is an important part of the reason for the mere existence of libraries, namely, to provide informational and recreational service to the full breadth of a particular library's materials. More often than not, in order to utilize this full breadth the publicizing, advertising, and general promotion of the library are vital. Public relations for libraries cannot be considered a lacy fringe that just as well may be trimmed away. Promotion of a service is not an admission that it is unimportant in itself, just as it is false that all products and services in the nonlibrary world are unimportant.

Look to the Experts

The techniques of the advertising trade play a highly significant role in moving our contemporary world. Librarians may not admire some of the birdbrained gems of Madison Avenue, but if they are to continue to offer their life work to the public along with an ever-increasing competition of attractions, they must pay more attention to some of the methods that work for the experts.

Our economic system is based largely on profit as the incentive for production. The dollar sign is our economic lighthouse. Some companies selling soaps, bleaches, toothpaste, mouthwashes, and cake mixes bring in tens of billions of dollars every year. Other companies reap $20 billion selling computers, or $60 billion selling cars and refrigerators and missile components. The Philip Morris conglomerate produces $45 to $50 billion each year hawking shredded plants in long white paper, chemicalized beer, sugary breakfast cereals, colored dessert gelatins, and machine-extruded cheese.

Profit to these companies means money, their definition in their terms. Without losing perspective, profit for us could be thought of in terms of library users. The equation of profits with people makes sense in the long run. After all, people are what libraries are for: to enlighten them, refreshen them, make them better citizens, better equipped to determine their own destinies, better persons.

If this is acceptable, librarians could learn from the experts. Procter & Gamble didn't bring in all those billions merely because it may produce the best bleach on the grocery shelf. Rather, it knows how to attract people to its products. It takes money and persistence and sheer gall to promote soap and toothpaste; and advertising agencies are the first to admit that despite all the intricate market research, they usually don't know the reason public relations works. They don't know for certain what triggers a response in a prospective customer. They can't predict a direct one-to-one causal relationship of what quality of response they may get in return for their messages, or the number of people responding, or the length of that response. What they do know for certain is that when the advertising stops, so do the sales. Fifty cents of every advertising dollar is wasted, goes the rule, but which fifty cents? Therefore, the effort of spending the full dollar is continued to ensure the good effect of one of these half-dollars.

All this is not to suggest that librarians should produce a stock of corny commercials that would make people shake their heads in disgust. It does mean, however, that we might benefit immensely from borrowing some of the successful techniques and axioms of the experts that are feasible and appropriate for libraries. One of the axioms of commercial advertising, for example, is simple: to elicit a significant response in a moderately intelligent person a message must be seen or heard by this person a minimum of six times; for a more intelligent person, three times. How many times have librarians thumbtacked a notice scrawled on a 3″ × 5″ index card onto a cluttered bulletin board to announce an open invitation for a special performance or gathering or display that the library is proud of? Is it a wonder no one shows up?

In an age in which knowledge, information, and research—not bleach and breakfast food—are the real fuels of our society, how much more significant a contribution libraries have to make, how much more ennobling their purpose. Neil Armstrong was not the first man to step on the moon because he drank artificial orange juice. He did so because of the phenomenal network of information and research that feeds the production lines of this country. Libraries are an intimate segment of this information network, but few laypeople are remotely aware of this. No company that had the slightest connection with the moon landing bypassed the opportunity to capitalize on its contribution. Librarians might pay attention to such broad-range institutional public relations. Such messages would place libraries in a more proper perspective and help build support for the future.

Librarians might make more people-profit by adopting some of the self-generated interest and loyalty that businesses are capable of producing. When so few outsiders toot the library horn, we should toot it ourselves. Continually. Enough times for all segments of society to hear, understand, and appreciate our message. Being important doesn't negate being in touch. Our libraries should be more of a contributing social force, and to accomplish this to full potential we need to promote what we have to those who don't know what we have. It isn't necessary to hawk our libraries, but it certainly is necessary to promote our products consciously and aggressively.

Public Relations in the Budget

In the commercial world promotion makes businesses bigger. At the same time, promotion is big business in itself. Advertising expenditures alone in a single year now amount to approximately $35 billion. Many of these huge corporations are selling canned peas, four-barrel electric toasters, floor polish, and miracle mouthwashes. What figures show how much libraries spend to promote a happier, better-informed life?

Certainly in terms of money, libraries are the greatest nonprofit institutions ever invented. Individual libraries budget extremely little, if any, money for promotion. If promotion brings in profits—for us, an ever-increasing number of better-informed, happier people—then libraries have much to accomplish.

Insurance carriers as a group spend the largest percentage of income for advertising—more than 10 percent of their sales. The average expenditure for general industrial groups is between 2 and 3 percent to promote their products. Some individual companies, however, spend much more. Procter & Gamble spends about 8.5 percent to urge us to buy more cake mixes. Revlon spends more than 10 percent of its sales on advertising its lipstick. Richardson-Merrell spends more than 15 percent advertising aspirin and other drugs. On the other hand, a library is fortunate if it has a separate line item in the budget for promotion of library services, let alone one percent.

Libraries are not companies, and efficiency of output and turnover are not the ultimate criteria of success. Nevertheless, to base the *raison d'être* of libraries, as many professionals still do, on the premise that knowledge need only be made available rather than used is a blue-ribbon rationalization. Our job is not merely to order and store materials and then describe this as making them available. We cannot justify our jobs by sitting back and waiting for the public to discover what treasures lie behind our doors. We must describe making-materials-available in terms of letting people know both before and during their visits to our treasure houses. This is a priority, and it should be recognized formally as a line item in any library budget, no matter how slight. A commitment to enlarging service will then have a solid, referable foundation on which to build an admired and useful future. Otherwise, if given the task, an outsider would find it difficult to justify the majority of library budgets in terms of the number of people served as against the money spent for acquisitions and keeping the plant open.

A Program, Not Just Publicity

Promotion of library services will not make libraries what they are not. Libraries are not movie houses, department stores, hardware stores, or even book stores. Yet an effective program of promotion, not merely occasional publicity on a whim, may indeed develop a lasting interest and fondness for libraries for what they can be to their patrons. Interest and fondness will lead to a continual use of their resources, which is the entire point.

Library promotion should also have its tributary motivations. The more skillful promotion is in attracting people to the library, the more activity is stirred in using it. The more people who use the library, the easier it is to justify its existence—and its budget. Greater demands must be satisfied by greater supply of services and materials. In fact, the demand for more services is the librarian's legitimate ammunition for requesting bigger budgets. More books must be provided for more readers. More records must be provided for more listeners, and more seats for more sitters.

We know that libraries of all kinds belong in the spotlight in our society. Let's get on with the work of making it happen.

2 What Makes Library Public Relations News

The service your library gives is its core. "Library" must translate "service" in the minds of the public or "library" will be that respectable place downtown that is seldom visited. Having on your shelves all the best-sellers in the world means little if they don't circulate. Including the most arcane reference books available is useless unless they are known and used. A new treasure added to your special collection isn't an El Dorado unless people see it and use it. If your library is indeed merely a respectable-place-seldom-visited and not more of a program of service, then it has slight justification for existing. When your few patrons pay more attention to the cracked paint on your walls than to the new photocopying machine for which you dredged your budget and twisted friendly arms, you have problems.

"Sure I want to promote the library," you say, "but I don't know what to promote."

Emphasize the New

Promote the new. In the extra-library world, the first move a company makes when it puts a new product on the market is to promote this product with a flurry of advertisements and commercials. The emphasis on promoting the new product is not given equal billing among the other company products but a highly disproportionate stress. The reason is that the chances for a new product to find its own way among the tens of thousands of competing attractions are minimal. Quite the contrary, it needs special pushing so that people become familiar with the name and concept of the new product as soon as possible.

Concentration of promotion at the outset is important. The surest way for a product to die on the shelf is to be ignored.

11

As a result, any substantial company moves its new products aggressively into the public mind, and if the product is good for them the paying public will buy and use it. Then its chances of becoming a staple and a habit are greater. Company chiefs know that no small measure for this success is derived from an intense program of promotion.

General Foods, for example, splashed the mass media with the good tidings of new Toast'Ems when this product suddenly appeared on the grocery shelves many years ago. The campaign was a success. (Somebody must think they're good.) Ford Motor Company developed its Mustang advertising fast and furious when the new model appeared in 1963, and ended up with one of the biggest success stories in Detroit history. Exceptions like the Edsel fiasco exist. Until recently, the Hershey Chocolate Company seldom advertised, relying instead upon superior packaging and product, plus word of mouth, rather than superior rhetoric for promotion. Nonexperts in promoting libraries, however, should pay attention to the rules, not the exceptions.

A first rule to borrow from the experts, then, is to promote new services—with heavy emphasis on "new." People are congenitally more curious about the new than the old. They want to know the latest political developments, the current fashions, the newest movies, the most timely advances in medicine. Promotion of something new is one of the best ways to spark interest in your library. Change (let's hope for the better) is news, and a new service means better service.

By all means, tell the story of your new color photocopying machine. Photograph it and post the prints at strategic points in the building. Print bookmarks that mention the new machine and insert them in books checked out at the circulation desk. Call the local newspaper to ask whether the editor is interested in letting the community know about this helpful new service that gives readers easy public access to one of the modern miracle machines. Promote the new.

Think Big

Thinking big should come naturally with such products as a new building or an addition to the old one or a revamping of the interior. However, you don't have to wait for big events to come along to think big. Think big with small events, too. The rest of the world realizes how effective this approach is. After all, how much importance may be attached to new toothpaste in the overall scheme of the cosmos? And yet millions of dollars in advertising are spent with deadly seriousness and an earnest heart to promote utterly simplistic concoctions.

If the experts make money-profit by thinking big with small events, it seems we librarians should pay attention and make people-profit with our own little projects. In many ways planned obsolescence is the keystone of the turnover of products. The ultimate in planned obsolescence is food, but a vast range of manufactured products in this country are carefully designed with get-old-quick qualities. Washing machines and automobiles are noted for built-in obsolescence. Then again, so are almanacs and newspapers.

One of the unabashed ways a company manipulates this artificial obsolescence is to develop new features of an old product. This way it may create a need in the owners of these goods to buy new models of the same product in order not to miss out on the latest company developments, small as they may be. It's an old trick. Car manufacturers advertise the advancement of hideaway windshield wipers over last year's model that—ugh!—merely leave the wipers in stark public view. Hideaway windshield wipers score a low mark on the overall scheme of modern transportation, but the industry never misses a chance to capitalize on the smallest item of change, of newness. In the fashion world the examples are obvious. An inch worth of change in either direction of belts and ties becomes the subject of huzzahs and headlines. It may indeed be ridiculous, but the fact is that this type of promotion helps move the production line into consumer hands and keeps a product turnover sprinting ahead on the treadmill to profits.

Libraries have immensely more to offer people than hideaway windshield wipers, thick belts, and thin ties. At the same time, libraries also have their share of small advances. Librarians should be aware that these may be stronger inducements to potential library users than the surface may suggest, especially if giving notice to these small steps for humankind are thought of in a big way.

The latest model of the *World Almanac* is structured basically the same as many previous models and contains basically the same information—except for one important factor. The latest model contains the latest information on the world production of crude petroleum, the latest information on the National League batting champion, the latest average price farmers in this country received for their products, the latest consumer price index, and scores of other up-to-date bits of information that weren't included in the previous model. Yet how many libraries have advertised the arrival of the latest *World Almanac,* even with a hand-painted sign on the front door?

"But a new *World Almanac* is really quite insignificant," you say.

So are hideaway windshield wipers. If hideaway windshield wipers and the latest petroleum information in the *World Almanac* are means of attracting people to the core of the matter, then they really aren't that insignificant. Rather, they're part of a program of promotion. Isolated, yes, they are of little value, but as a means of catching the curiosity of a segment of the general public, these small advances, new additions, and pieces of news, can be used to bigger advantage.

Think Public Relations

Without tuning your mental antennae to materials in your library that should be brought to the notice of patrons, without keeping your eyes open for new angles to bring notice to your library, even big projects will miss big thoughts. Think public relations in tandem with developing your new programs. Keep in mind that part of any major program is a strategy for involving as many outsiders as appropriate. Certainly a new library outreach program to low-income areas of the community, for example, is a major undertaking. Planning for promotion of the program once it's in effect must be integral from the beginning. Keeping city officials and other leaders informed on a continual schedule shows concern and competence. Then once the program is operating, publicity about what the library is attempting to do, what it has already accomplished, and what it plans to accomplish in the future most likely will draw more community support and participation. An encompassing promotion of such a program cannot afford to be overlooked. Yet many librarians do and later ask the reason the programs fail.

Major acquisitions by the library, such as a newly secured rare manuscript from a famous local author, are news and deserve public notice; they shouldn't be merely cataloged and forgotten. New best-sellers are always prime material in particular to promote the library in general. So is the addition of new seating space to accommodate the growing number of library users, newly found historical maps of the area, an unusual display of autographs, an important local painting on loan to the library for a month. Virtually anything different and new that has reference to your actual and potential clientele may be the subject of good promotion.

Perhaps none of the above examples, or your own, has relevance to your entire clientele. This doesn't matter. Almost nothing short of war and taxes has relevance to the entire public. What matters is that one segment of the populace will indeed take interest in a display of autographs, another in an historical map, and yet another in best-sellers. Fortunately, the world whirls this way. Not only this, but the library may perform one of its principal responsibilities—to help people find answers for their hearts and minds.

Ricocheting Rewards

An indirect benefit comes from putting the word "library" frequently into public view. Although no one may be remotely interested in a certain painting on loan to the library for a month, he or she at least may have seen mention of the library. "Important painting" becomes not as valuable as "library."

As usually happens, a general reference leads to a more personal one. Public mention of "library" in a certain context may lead individuals to what they consider a much more needful idea: "library" is a place to get a book on how to plant petunias or build a toolshed or find a novel or borrow a record or check out a book of poetry.

The point is that the rewards ricocheting off your promotion of a certain aspect of your library will not necessarily return directly. Publicizing a new painting exhibit does not mean that you should expect returns only by art lovers. This is the expansive nature of public relations. On the other hand, if no promotion is developed for the art exhibit, then the opportunity for reaping these indirect benefits is lost.

Behind-the-Scenes Tease

Another method to borrow from Madison Avenue is to open the doors a crack to the behind-the-scenes activities. A company often develops advertising campaigns that show highlights of what is being done to improve their products and services. This generalized, institutional-type advertising, as opposed to concentration on a single product, often finds a more willing reception. It is in the end merely one more angle to keep the public eye focused on the company. Opening the research door a crack appeals to the natural inclination in people to be privy to inside information.

No reason exists for librarians not to do something similar as part of their general promotion program. Perhaps a series of short profiles with photographs of your personnel and some words about how their jobs affect the public's use of the library might work for you. Or an annual open house during the end-of-the-year holidays for patrons to see how materials are processed in the back room.

Let the public know your plans and hopes and dreams about a better tomorrow for its library. If you plan to enlarge your film collection dramatically, let the public know not merely of the actual purchase but also your test thinking about it. Community reaction at the planning stage may help you decide either to enlarge the film collection further than you planned, abandon the expensive idea altogether, or detour its direction more to the public's liking. What matters is to be open. Welcome the community into some of your decisions for the future. You're the expert and you're hired to operate and maintain your library expertly, but they're the users. The community, whether it's civic, academic, or special, is, after all, the foundation of your library. The people you serve have a stake in what direction your library moves. Recognizing and allowing this stake to affect your decisions can only benefit you and your clientele.

If your community becomes more aware of what you're doing, and planning to do for them, then when a crisis arises, individuals will be more likely to be sympathetic to your situation. Having friends of the library won by giving them good service comes in handy when you have a leaky roof to patch or a bond issue to hatch. On the other hand, when the only time in the year the public hears of the library is during a crisis, it will be far less disposed to respond positively, and certainly not with the speed of someone who cares.

The Speaker's Formula

Use the speaker's formula of first telling the audience what you will be saying, saying it, and finally telling them what you've said. For example, you're planning a summer reading program devoted to science fiction. You let people know the date, time, and place of the program through posters in your library, articles about the discussion leaders in the school or city newspaper, and catchy excerpts from classic science-fiction books read on the radio. That's telling your audience what you plan to say.

Don't stop here. This is only one-third of the promotion mileage you can wring from a single program. Conduct your summer reading program on science fiction, but at the same time let other people know that right now is the time you're holding it. Put up new posters, send new articles to the newspapers, develop new radio spot announcements. Remind the people that what they heard a month before about the program is actually taking place right now, today. Others are enjoying it and they may too if they hurry to the library and sign up. This is the second ingredient of the speaker's formula.

When the program is finished at the end of summer, tell the public what you have done. This may be the first time some people will have heard of the program. It doesn't matter. They may be sorry they missed it. Next time they will pay more attention to what the library plans. If they see or hear in the future the word "library," they'll perk up so they won't miss something else appealing. Even the people who did join the series will like to read about what they attended. How many of us read the next day's newspapers about a concert or a football game or a news event we happened to see firsthand the night before? It happens all the time, and libraries should take advantage of the natural reaction and enjoyment in people. This is the third ingredient of the speaker's formula. Such follow-up promotion also maintains a record of what actually took place.

The Institutional View

Now and then give the public a look at the entire library field as a means of focusing on your own library. Let people know about ultramicrofiche and what it could do for the small branch library in your area. Let them know about the "house plan" for secondary schools that designs the library as an instructional materials center shared by each of the three or four separate high-school houses in one building complex; such a plan might save duplication of materials and money in your community. Tell people about cases of censorship in other states, and praise them for having a high regard for intellectual freedom and the First Amendment in their community. Tell them how satellites are vital to the development of library information networks across the country and around the world and that your particular community can be linked to this network to share the materials and resources of the great national libraries.

The People View

People are another important part in promoting libraries. People are interested in people, what they think, what they say, what they do. Star baseball players have no remotely conceivable relationship whatever to the quality of after-shave lotion, but people are interested in star baseball players, and this eases the way into the heart of the message. Actors contribute zero to the crunchiness of cornflakes, actresses

have nothing whatever in the world to do with the design of cars, but the public responds to familiar faces and waits for what they have to say.

Advertising agencies have known about this people-interest for decades on end and have exploited it to advantage. Libraries should do the same. Sign up baseball stars for endorsements if you can. In the meantime, don't feel that you are merely promoting yourself, that you or anyone else on the staff should remain out of the limelight. Yes, you yourself will get attention with your photograph and name in the newspaper or on television, but at the same time you will bring valuable attention to what you do and what you stand for.

Heads of multibillion-dollar corporations keep their companies before the public eye with periodic appearances and statements about their progress. In doing so, they refocus to a digestible image for the public the mammoth tangle of departments, processes, materials, and all the rest that constitute a huge company. Spotlighting a person as a representative of a company transforms the huge, vague, gangly conglomeration into human dimensions, making the hugeness seem accessible, approachable, and decent. Such public relations is subtle, indirect, and effective.

The next time you talk to the PTA about curriculum support, or to the freshman class on how to organize a bibliography, or to an ALA committee on outreach programs, by all means let other people in your community know what you're doing. The public will be interested in you, first as a person, and in turn as a librarian moving professionally into the social consciousness. You will distill the complexity of a library into accessible human terms so that the people may feel related to what you have to offer. A library is an abstraction, but you are a person as they are—and this is the true link. Seeing your name or picture or hearing your voice first of all as a person is the curiosity catch. After establishing this link, then you are identified as a librarian with a message to convey.

Let outsiders know that a member of your staff is traveling to such gatherings as a regional library conference. Public mention of this person first as a person, not an abstraction about the moral rectitude and honor of libraries, is an introduction to letting people know that librarians travel, that librarians are interested enough in their profession to learn

more about it, that librarians indeed have conferences, that
the information gained at these conferences is important to
the development of the people's library, that librarians are
looking out for the enrichment of others, and that where
there are people who happen to be thinking, traveling
librarians, there are also libraries with continuing futures.

You may be accused of promoting yourself or favoring a
certain few on the staff. This happens. Forget it. Pay attention
to what you know is your first purpose—promoting your
library. So you rock the boat a bit. Usually the ones who
complain don't pull the oars anyway.

What you're after is to bring notice to your library. Because
notice leads to action. And this is what you are ultimately
working toward: the action of more people using your library.

3 Developing the Library Image

Most people judge a complex reality by its simple substitute. The public thinks largely in terms of personal, institutional, and corporate images as a natural convenience. How people think of librarians and libraries is no exception. You and your particular library are no exceptions. In fact, your library has an image outsiders use in personal or social reference whether you work at it or not. If you don't work at it, the image may be stale and drab. It may need some polish and sparkle.

Adhesive Images

We all have our time-saving, diluted images of doctors in their white coats, lawyers in their courtrooms, cowboys on their horses. Railroads shoulder their monopolistic images of yesteryear. Oil companies manipulate their greasy tentacles all over the world. Congress is full of cagey opportunists. Images—prejudgments of groups we term prejudices.

These intellectual digests may be seeds of truth or germs of falsity. Whatever they are, these images of groups or institutions reflect reality in the minds of those who think them. They may attract people or repel them, encourage people or discourage them to respond favorably. Chemical companies focus on environmental issues to recoup a favorable public image. Automobile manufacturers proffer a new image of researching safety, the feasibility of electric cars, and other engine advancement to counteract a history of highway slaughter, air pollution, and high cost of energy.

Changeable Images

Corporations realize the significance of what outsiders think of their purpose and operations. They also realize that images can be changed. So should librarians.

21

At one time a "beer drinker" prompted the image of a tired brick hauler slouched in a ragged chair while he stared mindlessly at TV, slurped beer from the can in his hand, and wiped his mouth with the shoulder of his dirty T-shirt. The Brooklyn baseball team was known as the "Bums."

These images were changed consciously and radically. Today beer drinking is often associated with the high life on a yacht. The Los Angeles baseball team is known only as the Dodgers, never the Bums. The story of image making with the Dodgers, in fact, is a striking case in point. When the team was transferred to Los Angeles, the owners and sports writers joined in a deliberate, coordinated effort to never mention the "good ol' Bums" as they were known in Brooklyn. The agreement was kept and from the transfer day forward the team developed an image of the sleek Los Angeles Dodgers and nothing less.

Such an effort shows what may be accomplished for a public image. Once an image is embedded, it doesn't necessarily mean that the image cannot therefore be changed to fit not only the new situation but also the desires of the people behind the public image. From its inaugural issue *Sports Illustrated* set out to change the sporting image. It now makes baseball players, football players, wrestlers, and all the others what they aren't—clean, scarless, articulate Olympians who never sweat.

Changing Our Image

We know libraries already are run by clean, scarless, articulate Olympians who don't perspire. Does the public think this? Or does the public still think of libraries and librarians in the age-old stereotype that will not be repeated here?

In developing our public image, the most wonderful point to remember is that libraries and librarians have absolutely nothing to hide and everything to gain. A primary question to ask yourself is whether you wish your library to be part of today in order to serve as many people as possible. A library must be thought of as an integral part of the informational and recreational scene if it is to succeed in the face of all the other outlets for information and recreation in the modern world.

If this is how you think of your library, the next step is to convince the populace that a library is important to them today. The odds are not in favor of librarians. Most house-wives, plumbers, businesspeople, teenagers, government workers, real-estate brokers, dentists, and others still con-sider libraries as storehouses rather than distribution centers of information. The image by which these people prejudge a library must be changed if they are to be reached.

Thinking in terms of today, not eras past, is needed to develop an image of a library as being important to contempo-rary life. What is today? It's movement, it's faddy, it's media-oriented. It's intelligent, loose, colorful, and sexy. Inventive, electronic, futuristic, and fast. Frustrating, young, questioning, and rebellious. It's bewildering and beguiling. Your library doesn't have to be all these. Two or three will do.

The Need for Speed

Probably the greatest factor libraries have going for them is that people today want to know more and be entertained more. Mothers and fathers want to know about the latest experimental drugs, but they run out of time for researching the subject. Doctors want to know the latest findings about compounds that counteract leukemia, but they can't research all on their own. Biology students want the latest periodical article on synaptic transmission, high-school students want to know the cause of the explosion of the *Challenger* space shuttle on January 28, 1986, a shoe wholesaler wants to know the address of a potential customer in Detroit—now! They want this information immediately. Not in an hour, tomorrow morning, or next week.

People are used to getting what they want fast. Speed is no longer a twentieth-century luxury. Transistor radios and televi-sions speak up right away. Self-service banks eliminate waiting in line. Direct Distance Dialing eliminates waiting for tele-phone operators. People are simply used to being serviced fast. The world caters to consumers, but do our libraries?

People fill their days with innumerable activities, a reason, for instance, that parents don't have the time to wade through myriad articles on experimental drugs, even if they could locate them. They would rather forget the entire drudgery than bungle through the morass of publications in a library. Here's your chance. Help them. That's what you are there for. Don't wait to be asked. You seldom will be. Instead, be gently aggressive by bringing, for example, pertinent articles on drugs to the attention of parents by a public display. Then if you see or hear interest, ask if the people would like additional information. If they would, then photocopy an article or two and send the copies to their homes. This would cost a few pennies but reap much more good service, and image, in return. Save parents time. Save everybody time.

Doctors, biology students, and the others are included. Nearly everyone would rather drop the idea of muddling through a library in an eternal search for material when suddenly faced with the prospect. In their own minds time is precious and the flesh is weak. The effort librarians take to provide outsiders with fast information will be algebraically rewarded with appreciation and, more importantly, further use of an efficient, friendly library.

The job of providing fast information to our consumers helps nudge libraries further into the mainstream of American life today. To facilitate this a prominent information desk and telephone reference service are essential. What faster communication system is there than the telephone? Libraries should promote the use of telephone reference services during all open hours throughout the week and have it operated professionally and pleasantly. Make known through recurring memos, word of mouth, newspaper articles, signs in the library, that the simpler information may be had by simply dialing the library number. This makes libraries sourcehouses rather than storehouses, and librarians source points rather than sore points. Hordes of human bodies in a library building are not the ultimate measure of success, but answering the information needs of people is. If people today need fast information, whether it's to know if a book on brain tissue or the Bobsey Twins is available, then this should be given priority.

Accentuate the Positive

Thinking today is also thinking positively. We're living in an it's-possible time. Heart transplants, landings on the moon, televised pictures from Jupiter, laser beams, computers that work in nanoseconds, are part of our lives. Expansive thinking that comes with these marvels permeates ordinary lives. So think big. Accentuate the positive. If you want your library to share its importance among twentieth-century people, it can be done.

You are part of a unique profession. As a librarian you have no ulterior motive in the performance of your profession. A psychologist guides her patients according to her priorities. A social worker attempts to improve conditions according to his outlook and values. A doctor cures her way, a lawyer manipulates the law according to how he sees it, and a sociologist forms groups according to her theories. The patients and public usually have little say about these matters that intimately concern them.

On the other hand, a librarian is a singular creature. A librarian serves people according to their priorities and values and essential needs. If an individual wishes to read murder mysteries, then a librarian serves these needs. If another person searches for data on cryogenics of living tissue, a librarian serves these needs. The values and priorities of a librarian are totally on the side of the person served. Professionally, a librarian has no other reason to serve except to fulfill entirely the library needs of others. Only the librarian's expertise in locating materials to satisfy the patron's requests are brought forward in the transaction between librarian and user. Judgments are out. Do-gooding is taboo.

What a wonderful profession we have. In this age of service, more people should know more about libraries and librarians. Think positively about them, but think about them aloud.

Think Library

Experiment with passing the good word. Borrow ideas from other professions. A dentist's office is not an entertaining place for children to go. When youngsters visit a dentist, the atmosphere is made as inviting and ameliorating as possible. This way children won't have an abiding fear and abnormal uncomfortableness about having their teeth drilled when they grow into adults. What do dentists do to help this along? They pass out balloons or comic books.

Aldous Huxley suggested in *Brave New World* that books for children should be coated with sugar so that children would be predisposed to reading as they grew older. Libraries are probably not ready for this approach, but they should be ready to pass out balloons with "Think Library" on them to youngsters when they first come to the children's section. Perhaps a cartoon wall-hanging with "I Love Libraries" might be encouraging. Freely given, something-of-their-own gifts are effective. After all, how many grocery shoppers choose the brand with the jar designed to be later used as a glass, with secondary thought to the contents?

Adults shouldn't be neglected either. Don't wait for them to ask for a short list of notable books: slip one into a book they charge out at the circulation desk. Pass out calendars with library information on them. On the sly, give them some of the weeded books from the collection instead of trucking the old titles to the dump. Adults, too, need something concrete over and above a date-due stamp.

Think Service

Constantly think what libraries may give rather than what they may preserve. Once your new image catches hold, it's up to the living breathing real librarians to maintain the reality behind the sales pitch. The extended finger and proclamation, "Look it up in the catalog" remains more a fact than a cliché and should be forever banished. If people really knew how to use the card catalog, they wouldn't ask for help. No matter how obliquely they ask a question, the question wouldn't come up if it already had an answer. Sometimes these people need to be taught the use of the catalog, not to know where it is. Sometimes they merely need reassurance, to feel that the question has a possible answer and is not ridiculous, or need to share an interest in a subject with someone. Whatever, they want help from experts, who know what they're doing, who know how to save time, because, obviously, they do not. Librarians are specialists in the handling and utilization of libraries. Exploit this speciality to the fullest by conveying an unreserved sense that you enjoy helping others.

Today is an age of speciality. The speciality of the library is informational and recreational service—fast service, attractive service, accurate service. Liven up the surroundings with colorful signs. You don't need a $1-million bond issue to have large bright "Information" or "Card Catalog" or "Circulation" signs about the library. Have exhibits that illustrate today with subjects that are on the cover of recent issues of *Time,* not *Liberty Magazine.*

Library Environment

Pay attention to packaging. Learn about matching the environment of your library with that of your community, which presumes that you understand the community you serve. A library may be a pleasant, quiet, comfortable place to visit and still be in tune with the outside world. The front door of a library should not be an escape hatch but first of all an entrance.

If people in your community are at ease with loud signs, ultrafashions, and an electrifying world, make them at ease in your library, too. Time and again potential library users are rebuffed because the library appears standoffish, impersonal and isolated. Libraries function far more effectively without the Carnegie legacy of creating awe and hesitancy in outsiders. On the contrary, libraries need to create an environment that invites both smiles and questions.

This is not to say that a library should be an electronic shindig. A library, after all, is a place to study, to be alone, to read, learn, think, and dream. Yet it may also be a place to sit around and talk, to see a film, play a guitar, look at an art exhibit, listen to a panel discussion on space law. Rooms may be set aside for such activities. The entire building doesn't have to be entirely the same. People don't tiptoe anymore. A library is a place of communication. So make certain your patrons have the easy feeling that they may communicate in more ways than reading.

In the last analysis, developing an image of libraries and librarians rests upon certain principles of packaging and performance. Bright colors, fresh flowers, simple directions, pleasant people, comfortable surroundings, willingness to serve, smartness, style, simplicity, and smiles are not dishonest. They simply help promote libraries.

4   Know Your Product, Your Competition, Your Clientele

Nemo dat quod non habet: you can't give what you haven't got. You can't give forth enthusiasm for your library if you don't know about it. You can't give your patrons quick, accurate service if you don't know the inner gears of how acquisitions relates to cataloging and how cataloging relates to public service. You can't give potential library users the spark that ignites them over the threshold of reluctance if you don't have the spark yourself.

Libraries and librarians make their mark by helping to satisfy important intellectual and recreational needs in users, no matter at what level. This achievement is largely dependent on how much professional effort a librarian puts toward rich, personal service for a patron, service that not only meets the current needs of the people of a particular community, but also have enough vision to take a chance and anticipate future needs. This is the type of service that demands constant awareness both of the library field in general and of a working library in particular.

Know Your Product

The first training period for salespeople includes a thorough briefing and firsthand experience with the product they are assigned to sell to the public. While on the job they must be constantly informed of any modifications of their product or of new product lines within their company. "Know your product," they are told repeatedly. This way, appeals to the public imagination may be drawn from any number of possible angles to challenge the needs of any number of possible clients.

No less emphasis should come from librarians, especially when their product is vastly more complicated than the average commercial product, is an end result of the finest minds in history, and contains the seed-source of wonderment and uplift. Know your product and know it thoroughly. Leave no aspect of it untouched, even if you allow yourself merely a cursory awareness of an aspect of the field that tightens your abdomen even to think about. Establish a competence within yourself by knowing what is happening in the library field. At the same time establish a self-confidence by knowing what is going on within your own library as well.

Know Specifics

Gather together in your mind facts and figures and inspirational movements of your field. Know that at one time Ernest Hemingway was the most frequently translated author in the world, with ninety translations of his works into foreign languages. Know that the Library of Congress has more than 80 million items in 470 languages. Know that the research toward development of feasible optical scanners may have extraordinary impact upon the direction of your life's work and your patrons' needs and pleasures.

You may consider these bits and pieces of information as castaways for cocktail-party conversation, sequins that have no bearing on day-to-day transactions in your library. Nevertheless, they will be important when you talk with your teenage patrons about the significance of systems of knowledge. They will come in handy when you run across a pair of computer researchers and they mention that they are working diligently to create a thesaurus of terms without being aware that libraries have been using a subject-heading list for years.

Maybe a bright-eyed McLuhanite will approach you, the book custodian, with the triumphant admonition that books are on the way out and that electronic media will put your libraries out of business. Will you have to agree, or will you know enough about your product to say you've heard this threat for years. Then you may suggest possibilities he or she may not have heard of. Will you be up-to-date in knowing what adaptation and accommodation the library field is making in tandem with less expensive computers, faster automatic typewriters, satellite relays?

You might say that the 1,246 pages of the Bible have long been reduced to a two-inch-square piece of film and that ultramicrofiche promises greater advances in hard-copy knowledge storage. You might say that, on the contrary, book production is increasing, not decreasing, and that people with minority, specialized interests have a much greater chance of finding book and periodical information than ever before; publishers specializing in books for select markets are prospering, not going out of business. Printed matter is indeed far from a cul-de-sac invention. Already automatic book page-turners are used in hospitals for patients unable to use their hands. Microfilm may be used in a similar way. Who knows?

You might suggest that cable television is the first step toward developing a widespread two-way system of communication between home and library. Cable TV in libraries, like telephones in libraries, provide the first real opportunity for home viewers to turn their homes into surrogate libraries. "Besides," you may say to the startled McLuhanite, "whatever made you think libraries are restricted to only books? Libraries are not book centers. They're information centers."

Move Around

Most of all, wander around your library. Don't get stuck in your slot. Get to know your library as intimately as you can. If your library is alive at all, it changes. Keep up with these changes so you can tell your patrons about them.

Make a habit of examining the new book shelf. Be aware not only of what new titles are being published but also of the titles that your individual library has on its shelves. That's what is important to a reader: not so much that a favorite writer has a new book out but that your library has it ready and waiting to be borrowed. Mentally pick out titles that might appeal to patrons you know and then, the next time you visit with them, suggest that they might like to read them. Let people know that you're looking out for their welfare.

Know what is in your periodicals and newspapers. Only a few minutes a day are needed to browse through the periodical section. Glance through the feature articles that seem to have good general appeal. If your library subscribes to foreign or national newspapers, remember some of the principal articles in the *Japan Times, The* [London] *Times, New York Times.* Do so with the thought that this is part of your professional calling. You're remembering these articles for your patrons' sake, not yours alone.

Know what is in your display cases and on your bulletin boards at all times. Some librarians hardly pay attention to their own shop. Nothing reveals a lack of interest in your work quite so fast as to have someone come up to you and ask about the display of local jewelry making: "Well," you have to answer, "to tell you the truth, I didn't know we had a new display up." What can the patron do but say, "Oh," and walk away?

Wander periodically through the receiving room of the acquisitions department. This gives you a chance to talk to people here and to discover interesting titles when they come in. By knowing what new titles the library recently received you can mention them to readers you know have related interests. "I just saw a new book out on extrasensory perception; it came into the receiving room yesterday," you can say. "I'll reserve it for you, if you like?" Nine times out of ten you have sold a title and gained a friend for the library.

Don't let your new reference works sit on the shelf and collect years instead of use. Know and use them. Know what new music and speech records arrived. Thumb through *Vital Speeches* to be aware of what important addresses are included so that you may mention them to certain patrons who would like to see more than what is usually excerpted in newspapers.

Visit the departments in your library to be aware of what is going on in your own building. Get the big, overall picture. Know the people you work with. Know your colleagues. Read your professional journals. Know what's happening in your field. Know what's happening in your library. It's simple: know your product.

Know Your Competition

No one is born to use your library. Competition in the modern world for an individual's time and money is fierce.

More outlets to take up the slack of leisure time are available to Americans than ever before. At least 98.2% of American households have one television set—91 million screens, 87 million of them color sets, and most of them are operating an average of seven hours a day with programs from 1,362 stations around the country. More than 99% of the households have radios, filling the air from 4,392 AM stations and 4,155 FM stations. More than three times as many billions of dollars are spent on toys and sports equipment than on books. Attendance at national league baseball alone numbers 53 million people. Tens of millions of phonograph records and compact discs are played. Tens of millions of transistor radios are carried instead of books. The spreading use of videotape recorders (53 million used now) is usurping still more time from your library.

True, 47,000 book titles are published in this country each year, and more than 800,000 backlist titles from 30,000 publishers in the U.S. are available. Yet this reflects only a fraction of the focus and time people could spend on books, the mainstay of libraries.

Seldom a Dull Moment

Americans are active people. They're doers, travelers, participants, spectators. They're time-fillers and learners. They're mechanical wizards, inventors, and hucksters. They're constantly promoting new ways of doing old things. They're constantly devising new products and services to keep their economy on the move. Seldom is there a dull moment on the American scene, and if there is one, it is usually at a stoplight.

The time they spend in their cars is time away from your library, more than one trillion vehicle miles of it a year. The time spent on recreation of one sort or another is time away from your library. Tens of millions of people fill the race-tracks, bowling alleys, baseball stadiums, football stadiums, golf courses, and basketball courts. This doesn't include the millions who participate or watch the other popular sports, such as tennis, swimming, softball, yachting, fishing. The list goes on and on.

Rechanneling the Energy

All these activities have their importance, but it is obvious that while these millions upon millions of Americans are involved in so many of these forms of recreation, whether in the field or watching on TV, they are not at the library. Perhaps this is as it should be. On the other hand, it is most likely that many of these people do not realize the benefits available from the 8,455 public library systems, 4,125 academic libraries, 5,287 special libraries, and the rest of the 29,460 libraries around the country.

Psychologists tell us that, given the right motivations, the natural energy in people may be channeled in nearly any direction. The energy is inside, the motivations outside. This energy may go entirely into weekend sports and weeknight television. Or it may go into weekend sports and weeknight activity at the library learning how to improve a knuckleball. It may go into watching a Thursday-night television boxing match or into a library book on the art of politics.

Librarians would do well to learn to compete with and complement the other outlets of leisure and information. The first step in this competition is to understand and appreciate the many avenues people face in choosing what to do with their time. Television and movies have an overwhelming attraction value and that once general life patterns settle into daily routines, the inertia of a set behavior is difficult to overcome. Be aware that an individual sometimes confronts far more time-wasting activities than time-consuming.

At the same time, know that, given the right stroke of intellectual lightning, the same individual may be persuaded that knowing more about fishing is more profitable than not knowing more. Where do you find more out about fishing? It's up to you to provide this potential library user with the opportunity to think at least once of the library.

This is called meeting your competition. The third step in the selling chain is equally if not more important:

Know Your Clientele

Salespeople never really sell to complete strangers. Neither should librarians deal with an unknown patronage. Learn from the specialists. Study the full breadth of your potential clientele. What are their ages? Their major interests? Their minor interests? Their discretionary time? Their education, income, family size? You may not be able to afford a formal study, nor be inclined toward one, but at the minimum sit down, pull out a few records, talk with other librarians, and come up with some profile. An approximate profile is better than none at all because it is something in hand to improve. Whatever the outcome, setting aside time to assess your clientele methodically and consciously forces you to pay attention to understanding the people you are supposed to be serving. It also helps you understand the general interests and motivations of the people who now use your library and gives an indication of those you wish to reach. By keeping these interests and motivations uppermost in your mind, you're on your way to soaking the most mileage from the services you offer.

One cue that can't be ignored is the undying American characteristic to better ourselves. A library flourishes under this characteristic. Also, a library should contain material in all three basic media formats—print, film, and electronics. These are what modern Americans are familiar with, and they should see them in their libraries. They will connect with an energy in your library because they themselves are energetic. In a similar way, they'll feel more attracted to your library and more comfortable visiting it if they see rooms set aside for discussion, record playing, film showing, because they see and use these in their own homes and community.

The Five-Part Life Span

Understanding some of the basic tenets of psychology helps in meeting the needs of library users, attracting new ones, and maximizing the return from the time and effort that goes into a modern library. Generally, psychologists divide the active life span into five parts: childhood (3–13 years), adolescence (13–20), young adulthood (20–40), middle age (40–60), and old age (60–death).

Librarians should know that children live in a tree-talking world where mystery and wonder are forever present to

discover. Intense imagination and anthropomorphism fill the
young child's world. Nearly every activity is a discovery
period. First impressions are vivid and deeply meaningful.
The world may have existed for eons, but to children it was
born only yesterday. They carry on dialogues with cats and
dogs and it's all perfectly coherent. Children become more
mighty than we can now imagine. Doesn't the sun follow
them around when they run and look over their shoulders?
Couldn't they see the flowers pick themselves if only they
could lie and wait long enough? Why is it so much fun to learn
new things?

(Shouldn't the library for children be full of the same wonder?)

Teenagers are something else again. They're unsure of
themselves. They're caught between the devil and indepen-
dence, and they aren't quite certain which direction to turn.
They're not yet adults and they're not still children. They're
impetuous and attention-getting. Life problems take on
monumental importance. What is sex all about anyway? What
jobs are most appealing? Why do adults say one thing and do
another? Why do adults speak to them as if they were
children? What is love? What is truth? Won't somebody be
honest for a change?

*(Librarians must be ready to meet adolescents honestly and be
sensitive to the fact that they seek more answers than they have
questions for.)*

Young adulthood is often described as the prime of life.
Men and women have reached full physical and intellectual
development and are usually active to their fullest degree.
They are involved in their work and marriage. They are
building for the future. Yet they often meet with debilitating
frustrations: people in business cannot find spare time;
modern housewives need outlets to develop their creativity
and education. In one way or another they all strive for
personal identity and fulfillment. Their loves take on deeper
meaning and often become absolutely essential to their
achievements. They seek status and success, but they also
seek answers to the more profound questions of life.

*(Libraries must be flexible enough to meet these needs of highly
specialized informational requests as well as to satisfy the deepest
desires of personal quests.)*

On the other hand, middle age may be the apogee of life, the time of leadership that favors the answers over the questions. This is generally the period of the largest income and greatest security. It is an active period, although illness, age, and mental slowdown become more probable. Men and women of this age period find themselves asking whether or not they have done right with their lives. They look back on their younger motivations and sometimes smile at themselves. They wonder if they have contributed anything. They wonder why they didn't achieve more.

(*In terms of influence and professional achievement and satisfaction, good library service to this age group often brings in more than is given out.*)

Old age may be a time of leadership for some, too. Generally, however, men and women of this period look toward retirement. They often blossom into second childhood. They slow down and let their life take a decidedly leisurely pace. Death becomes a recurring mystery to ponder. They remember the better days when they didn't have physical infirmities and when life still had far more to offer than take away. They could become involved in more activities, but they usually figure the effort isn't worth it in the long run. They would rather concentrate on the exquisite things of life, the little achievements that only older people have the patience to accomplish. After all, they've been where everyone else is going.

(*Librarians with patience and friendliness may find this age period extremely delightful and usually very appreciative.*)

Librarians might make greater headway toward an encompassing success by being more aware of some of these basic human needs and motivations that appear before them in those with shiny bright faces, those with acne, those with determination, those with satisfaction, those with wrinkles. The fascinating continuum of human life presents librarians with challenges few others have the opportunity to confront. So know your clientele. Know the people you serve. Love them. How else can you be a good librarian?

PART TWO

5 Campaigning for Funds

Directors of tax-supported libraries are finding that they and their trustees must look for sources of funds other than the traditional channels. Marketing for money has become especially important to an increasing number of public libraries supported by taxpayers with ever-expanding demands for other services. As a result, many libraries are being forced to curtail their services, institute user fees for special categories, cut back on the purchase of new materials, or request fantasy increments of their budgets that will never be granted. All this makes it necessary to look toward other horizons for money.

The trustees of the Keene (N.H.) Public Library campaigned for money in a way that many public libraries will do in the future. They went hunting for money not for a new building or a new wing but for new books—for intellectual expansion. Their highly successful example is instructive for what they learned, how they appealed to prospective donors, and how they conducted their campaign. They showed how good public relations were not only the foundation but also a power source of their fund drive. This is how they did it.

Quantifying the Needs

When library space is short, usually the public can see it with their own eyes. Books are stuffed into the shelves like clothes in a discount shop. Quiet reading space is lacking, furniture is worn and scarred, study carrels and periodical room chairs and tables are in skimpy supply.

On the other hand, when a book collection is old and out of date, the need to upgrade it may not be as obvious to the patrons. Some readers will notice that entries in the card or computer catalog are behind the times, and that the most checked-out titles and other materials are worn and frazzled. On the whole, however, for most people, and for the greatest impact, it's important to assess the collection and put the need into clear numbers, and to back them with authority. This is how the Keene (N.H.) Public Library began its campaign.

Although a new building addition to the century-old library was completed in 1980 and doubled the physical size, the book collection itself failed to match the new space with new titles. With the completion of the new physical space, the trustees had accomplished a major goal. But what was needed for the 1980s and 1990s? By 1985 four basic objectives were developed. Upgrading the book collection was paramount (after creating public awareness of the library, giving the staff more training, and moving into automation).

To quantify the first priority, Jane Perlunger, director of the library, initiated a study of the book collection and its deficiencies. A second study was conducted by the New Hampshire State Library. The two studies concluded that the Keene Library needed to purchase 19,000 books. At the then average price of $28 per title, this meant the trustees had to find $600,000.

Quantifying the Services

At the same time, putting some of the services into numbers was done. This put the Keene Library into perspective as a service agency to the community. More important, these numbers of positive services were to be used later when volunteers approached prospective donors so that they could paint an easily-grasped numerical picture of how well the 83,000-volume library had been doing under the circumstances.

These are the numbers that the Keene Public Library used: 11,000 area adults and children hold current cards; more than 180,000 books and materials are lent each year; more than 10,000 visits by patrons are made to the library each month; more than 75 children attend reading or story groups each week; more than 30 inquiries for information are fielded every day.

Other services of libraries are sometimes impossible to put into numbers—but most people can't ingest too many statistics at one time anyway. So this allows qualitative services to be listed in conjunction with the above categories. The Keene Library, for example, received two grants for a literacy program in a city that is much concerned about reading ability. An outreach delivery system of books to nursing homes, shelves of large print books, summer reading programs for children, and reference services by telephone are among other services it is important for people to know about.

The point is to gather and delineate the services your library provides. Do this early in the book enhancement fund campaign so that you not only understand your needs but also your virtues.

Public Money

The first stop that a public library normally makes en route to more money is city hall. This is what the trustees of the Keene Public Library did, but the city manager hemmed and hawed at the sight of $600,000 on the bottom line. The scene is familiar to most large and small public libraries.

The city manager, however, suggested an alternative—a private sector/public sector challenge in a joint financial relationship. As a result, in 1988 the trustees accepted the challenge of raising half the money from the business and industrial community and private citizens of the city of Keene. The basic plan was that every dollar the trustees raised the city would match. If your library is in a similar situation, you might consider making the challenge to your city manager instead of waiting in hope for him to make it.

Feasibility Study

As with most public libraries, the Keene Library never had raised outside money before. It relied on the annual public monies for its entire budget. The first matter at hand was to

form a six-member Library Campaign Committee that would
focus its attention on the job, organize volunteers, and
conduct the fund drive. Phil Faulkner, energetic and knowl-
edgeable about the sales and marketing world, was named
chairman. He was recently retired and had time to devote to
the challenge.

"We weren't too sure of ourselves," he said, "so we hired a
consultant to do a feasibility study. He came back and said,
yes, you can raise $300,000, the public is receptive to that.
But it's going to take a period of over five years to collect it."

After this report, the trustees decided formally to go ahead
and proceed with the campaign. The decision was made in
August 1989. The outside study gave the trustees confidence
that at the minimum residents of the community felt favorably toward their public library and that the trustees were not
barking up the wrong tree. Signs were indeed evident that the
request of the library wouldn't be met with hoots and hollers,
and damage the future image of the library.

Big Money First

One of the axioms of searching for substantial amounts of
private money for a project is to aim for large donations first.
Raising money from neighborhood residents can work, but
this is an expensive way to raise money. The ratio of small
gifts to the large number of mailings and telephone calls
increases the time, work, and administrative costs.

In view of this, the Keene Library trustees outlined a
four-level scheme of priorities of prospective donors: (1) the
trustees themselves; (2) business/industry; (3) leadership
individuals; (4) community.

The trustees concluded that if the campaign and they
themselves were to be credible and successful, they would
need to make substantial gifts themselves, and they must be
the first to give, which they did. The business/industry and
the major leadership levels would be approached personally
by the trustees and volunteers. The community level of the
campaign would be done by mailings. All the gifts would
come from within the city limits.

Brochures and Printed Matter

Whenever a prospect for a gift is approached, leaving some printed matter is important. If a gift is not decided upon immediately, the prospect then has a brochure or flyer on hand as a reminder or something tangible to study privately. Also, it's important for a campaign committee to provide material to volunteers whose task it is to approach the prospects. They too need material to remind them of facts about the library and approaches to make when they meet the prospects.

The Keene trustees designed such material. For the twenty volunteers, they printed two how-to-do-it flyers. The first was a two-page "Successful Campaigning" instruction outline of procedures and suggestions on how to approach prospects. The second three-page "Presentations to Prospects" outlined some major points about how the Keene Public Library serves the community and significant historic events and dates that have brought the library to the present. This flyer was designed to inform the volunteers so that they were comfortable with the background of the library and could discuss it with ease and confidence.

The brochure for the general public was an eight-page 6" × 9"-inch publication attractively but simply designed and printed. This would be used as a surrogate in-person volunteer, and therefore it had to look confident and be professional. This would be one of the principal links of public support and had to toe the line between conveying need and appearing extravagant. The brochure was designed with black and white photographs of simple scenes in the library—a librarian reading a story to floor-sitting children, a close shot of an open catalog drawer, a shot of four tattered books, the painting of the "philanthropic, community-minded spirit of Edward Thayer who made this library possible by his generous gift in 1898," and other photos. One large photo to a page. Short paragraphs of text. Big, easy-reading type. Lots of white space. In short, an informative, quickly-grasped description of the library and its needs. And, of course, the main thrust of the brochure was not shirked. In bold type it stated, "Every dollar of private support will be matched by the City

of Keene." This was printed next to the page that told "How
to Make a Gift" and how donors would be commemorated on
a plaque placed prominently in the library. But this was not
the end, not the message that the trustees left as the bottom
line. A library, after all, has a different bottom line. The next
page of the brochure described the hope and focus of what
these gifts would bring—"New Ideas. New Directions. New
Books."

Anticipate the Negative

Before approaching the prospects for gifts, prepare yourself (and the volunteers) for reasons why they should *not* give
to the library fund. Take their point of view. This will help
you solidify your side of the story as well as prepare you to
answer their questions ahead of time. This way you won't end
up fumbling for an answer when you're in their office or
home.

List the questions on a piece of paper. They might include:
Why should I give when I already pay my taxes? I don't live in
this city so why should I give? If I give now, will you come
back in ten years and say the library is in bad shape again?
Why doesn't the city pay for all of the budget? What do I get
out of this donation? Why are you asking me? How much of
this money is used for administration? Will this increase city
taxes?

Approach the Positive

The Keene Public Library trustees decided in clear terms,
for their own benefit, to relate the importance of the library
within the community. They chose to try to strike a chord
with anyone they were approaching for a donation through an
understanding of the prospect's interests. For instance, the
library was very active in the literacy campaign. So when some
prospects in town were known to be similarly interested, the
trustees focused on this interest in their presentations. Others
were interested in the children's program that the library does

well; the trustees focused on this aspect for this particular group. The point may be obvious when articulated, but sometimes the obvious isn't clear until it's articulated. It's good to make such approaches crystal clear before proceeding with any campaign.

Faulkner gives example of how he approached certain groups. First, he established that, yes, the library did set a good purpose in the community. Next, he talked about the two studies made of the book collection needs and what was discovered about updating the material. Then he spelled out the money needed and the matching challenge with the city designed to accomplish this.

He was a member of the Rotary Club; his brother belonged to the Lions Club. As one of its overall programs, the Lions Club is interested in eyesight conservation. The Rotary Club goes for anything related to youth. "I went to both of them," he said. "At the Lions Club I explained the campaign and said we need more books, especially more large print books. 'Oh, boy, that's right up our alley,' they said, 'Great,' and gave us $7,500. Then I went to the Rotary Club and explained the same thing, showed them the children's geography books that were out of date, and said we need more children's books. They said, 'Great,' and gave us money."

Show and Tell

Demonstrate needs. Go through your collection and pull out books from the shelves that are specific examples of what you're talking about.

Phil Faulkner did it this way. He used only three books to create a vivid impact, but he picked a rounded selection. One volume was a short story collection of classics. It had been checked out so many times that it was totally worn out. Pages were missing, the binding was falling apart. His second example was a popular children's book titled *Having Fun with Geography,* written in the early 1950s. He read excerpts from the book that referred to the 48 states and said that most countries in Africa were controlled by other countries in Europe. Then he pointed out that if the youth of Keene read that today, they'd be much out-of-date and uninformed. This was not the way to educate our young people, he emphasized. His third example was a book on computers written in 1979. The book was only eleven years old, but it was completely beyond its prime. This showed that although a book may be relatively new, a patron reading certain subjects, especially in science and technology, can be out of touch with the times.

Then, to enlarge the impact further, he said, "We have hundreds more like these. We need to replace these books."

Success

For each request from a potentially major donor, trustees and volunteers of the library made personal appearances. They always telephoned for an appointment, arrived on time, made their presentation, and called back if necessary. The presentations averaged about twenty minutes. Most prospects made the decision on the spot.

"Our approach," Faulkner said, "was this. If you are interested in the library, would you consider a pledge of $1,000 a year for five years, for a total of $5,000? That's the way we asked for it. We didn't use any pressure tactics. We just made the suggestion. If they couldn't do that but wanted to give some, we let them come back with a figure. After all, they're the ones who can determine what they can give."

In times of a weak economy, some people in your own campaign may have to give less than they would at other times. So you may wish to lower the asking figure. On an individual donor basis, however, you'll likely face little difficulty.

In the end, the Keene Public Library Campaign totaled $307,000 by June 1990 and ended the drive sufficiently beyond the matching challenge. The final breakdown was enlightening. The biggest bracket of giving was in the $1,500 to $2,000 level by individuals. The range of gifts stretched from $5 to $50,000. One gift was for $50,000, there were two for $20,000, one for $15,000, one for $12,500, and three for $10,000.

The pledges in money broke down this way:

Trustees and friends	$62,000
Major gifts (business/industry)	$185,000
Leadership individuals	$60,000
TOTAL:	$307,000

The number of pledges were: Trustees, 22; Major, 20; Leadership, 67, for a total of 109.

The drive was planned and conducted so well, and with such good public relations, that the fourth level of prospects—the ordinary community residents—never needed to be approached.

Follow Up

Before and throughout any campaign, try to place articles and reports in the local newspapers, and on radio and television. But don't forget after the campaign is closed. Reports of success are always legitimate subjects of news, and the Keene Library trustees took advantage of this opportunity to keep the name and idea of the library in the public mind.

For the volunteers a victory celebration was held, providing a chance for these workers to pat each other on the back. For the donors, every individual or business that donated $10,000 or more was given the opportunity to honor somebody with a book plate in three hundred of the new books bought. During the campaign, this possibility provided some incentive to give $10,000. One family, for instance, did so for a child who died in a motorcycle accident. A dozen individuals or families made use of this option.

In addition, all who gave $1,500 or more had their names on a plaque at the library entrance. They were divided into four categories according to the size of the gift.

Evaluation of the Campaign

Once a campaign is finished, sit back and examine how well or badly it went. Whether you conduct the same kind of campaign in the future or not, the points you learn may be applied to something different.

For instance, the Keene trustees thought about what did not work. Not much, except for some unfortunate timing that was based, fortunately, on underestimating the generosity of the city support for the library. Success is often the result of a small campaign and wise counsel. The Keene trustees did, in fact, listen to their consultant, whom they learned about through other successful campaigns he had advised on for the Red Cross and the Boy Scouts in New Hampshire. The fund-raising consultant told the trustees that the further they got away from the six-member Campaign Committee, its work, and the personal contacts they had in the community in soliciting the gifts, the weaker the presentation would be. He told this core group that they themselves would probably raise two-thirds of the money. This turned out to be true.

An important long-range point is implied here. Many library board members are selected not with the idea that they are going to have to raise money. On the other hand, if someone belongs to an art gallery or museum board, part of the function of that membership *is* to raise money. These people are selected for the board specifically for that reason. But normally a library board member is selected by a mayor on appointment and verified by a city council. These people may be interested in the library, but are they people who can raise money? This question should be addressed early on.

Cost

Gifts of money cost money. A mark of a successful campaign is to keep the costs low. Some campaigns can cost in administrative and material expenses up to twelve percent of what is raised.

One way of reducing the cost that would go to outside paid workers is to count on doing much of the work yourself, which is what the Keene Public Library trustees did. "We were a bunch of Yankees," Faulkner said, "so we tried to save money where we could." The cost of raising $307,000 for the library ran to $15,000, below five percent.

One of the factors that contributed to this low cost was early success from the pledges from large donors. The trustees did not have to approach the smaller community prospects for $25 and $50. This expensive way of raising money, involving much labor and postage, might have cost up to twenty percent of what was raised.

In fact, the printing of 700 brochures was designed for mailing to the community level prospects. Five hundred brochures were never used in this way. Eliminating those would have saved money, if only the trustees had known that the campaign for the major gifts would be so successful and so quick.

Have a Good Product

An important reason why the Keene Public Library now has enough money for new books is that the community it serves has long considered its library helpful, well-run, well-trained, easy and comfortable to use. In other words, it enjoyed long-term good public relations. Otherwise, it wouldn't be likely that the library, which once purchased 4,000 books a year, could for the next four years double the number of books normally bought.

"One of the things that made the campaign important and fun," Faulkner said, "was that, first of all, people thought highly of the library. We weren't getting, 'Well, I don't like the library.' One of the things that gives you the greatest satisfaction is when people give you money and they feel good about it. We had people who gave us some big money and were so pleased to be able to do it. We had somebody give us $5000 and say, 'I just enjoy giving you this money. It gives me the greatest pleasure to give you $5000, I want you to know that. I'm so glad I'm in a position to do this.' Well, this brings tears to your eyes."

Another aspect that provided a strong incentive was the concept of a matching challenge—the public and private sector uniting to solve a community problem. "For every dollar you give, the city matches it," Faulkner said. "That had a lot of appeal."

The lesson is clear: If you don't have a good product, you're not going to sell it. If your library is not well thought of, you'll have a tough time getting New Ideas, New Directions, New Books.

6 Campaigning for a New Building

Developing a new library building or an extension is one of
the most difficult challenges a professional encounters. Such
a project devours countless hours of discussion, decisions,
details, and drudgery. Architectural plans must be understood and accepted, supervising authorities have to be educated and convinced, the normal flow of library service
becomes distracted and unsettled.

But a major concern, especially for public libraries, is
presenting the new concept to taxpayers and igniting interest
and enthusiasm. Without broad-based support for a new
building, the years of working for the building could collapse
in a fraction of the time it took to mount the project. Here is
what the Wellfleet Public Library on Cape Cod, Massachusetts, did to help insure its success.

The Old Story

For 95 years the Wellfleet Public Library had been situated
on the second floor of the Town Hall. This was sufficient
space for a small library in a small town of a couple of
thousand people in winter, although the population swelled
to startling numbers in the summer. Over the years, however,
library needs expanded and available space dwindled. By the
late 1970s and early 1980s, the shelves were jammed to the
limit. Books were stored in cartons at the end of the stacks
while other books were stuffed horizontally on top of those in
the shelves. Staff space for working turned into a maze of
obstacles. Periodical storage space was bulging, quiet study
areas for patrons were nonexistent. The 2000-sq. ft. library
grew to 25,000 volumes in a shelf space sufficient for only
13,000 volumes. It was an old story. The library was outgrow-
ing its location, reaching the point of no return, almost literally.

52

The staff, in fact, tried to keep as many books in circulation as possible so they wouldn't take up space in the library.

The trustees saw the writing on the wall in 1977 and approached the selectmen (the town officials), who agreed to appoint a Library Building Committee to search for a new site. Supporters and users of the library were largely in agreement that a new building was needed, but many others in town had to be convinced.

Dual Endeavors

Two main directions were undertaken. The first was to generate interest among the townspeople that a new library was absolutely needed, and to predispose them to vote for the funds for construction. The second was the behind-the-scenes work of preparing the complicated plans and long-term schedule for presentation to the town authorities.

A search for a building site ended up with every possibility eliminated for one reason or another. Either the site was too far from the village center and therefore would diffuse the cohesion of town services, or a site that might have worked had been sold in the interim. Some sites were too expensive, others could not be reconverted to accommodate parking of cars. The best site turned out to be a semi-abandoned former candle factory in the town center. By the time this site was determined to be the best of the lot, eight years had passed.

In the meantime, the town had built a new fire station and a new school; a water supply and a solid treatment projects were coming up for consideration—but they weren't quite ready yet. "So we knew we had to move," said Elaine McIlroy, head librarian and leader of the new library project. "What we did was to get an appraiser for this site, and then we negotiated with the owners. We had an architect we'd been working with give us an off-the-cuff figure for renovation. The figure we came up with was $1.3 million for the purchase and renovation. We kind of took a back-door approach. But here was the site, with a building already on it—and time was fleeting. We had this window of opportunity that a couple of big projects had been paid for, and others were pending for the next three or four years.

To build citizen support, McIlroy, her staff, and volunteers took the plans to civic groups—school committees, the South Wellfleet Neighbor Association, and open hearings. All the facts and problems were placed in clear and frequent public view: the money involved, how it would be financed, and what the town would be getting for the money. Some people questioned the choice of renovating a 1930 wooden building when for $1.3 million a new brick building could be constructed. The librarians had done their groundwork well and could show that all reasonable possibilities were exhausted— no one knew where to build a new library. Renovation was the sound choice.

During all this time, news and feature articles in the newspapers were published. Some were initiated by the librarians, some by the editors. Once McIlroy approached the *Cape Codder* editor to write an editorial supporting a new library; the attempt wasn't successful, but later the editor assigned an article on several nearby towns with outmoded libraries, including Wellfleet. "The newspaper articles were strung out for years before we finally asked for money," she said. "No one was in the dark about what we wanted to do. Sometimes these things come out of the blue, but ours was no surprise to anybody. They knew something was going to be proposed someday. By letting people know what the problem is, they would say to us, 'Oh, finally, it's about time, you've waited so long.' So in general it was better to let people know ahead of the vote."

Preparation for the Vote

In Massachusetts a small town budget is ultimately determined by town meeting vote of residents in attendance, not by the town officials. Article warrants are listed and read aloud, and a particular issue or budget item is discussed before the town meeting vote is cast yes or no. Although it was important to have the support of the selectmen town officials (which at first did not happen), the library staff and volunteers absolutely had to have the support of the people sitting at the meeting.

This meant that support and passage of the vote to acquire the site and its subsequent financing for renovation depended on having as many library supporters at the town meeting as possible. Clearly, the Library Building Committee needed to pack the house.

"We had to get all our supporters to attend the town meeting," McIlroy said. "The Friends of the Library got together and phoned people to come out and support the library. You just have to get your supporters to be there and speak for you." (The Friends and Volunteers starred names on the town voting list who were known to be library users and who were likely to support the project; these likely supporters were called on the phone and urged to attend.) "And those people did come out for four nights," she said, "because we had to wait to present our warrant article. We did a lot of active work, we really did reach out, because we couldn't be sure of the vote."

Other means of getting out the voters included sheets of background information mailed to every household prior to the town meeting. The information was typed and designed for quick and easy reading. It contained sections such as "Why Does Wellfleet Need a New Library?" (Answers spelled out that library use had increased 800% but space only 10%, volumes increased from 6,068 to 25,000.) "What Sites Have Been Considered? Why Discarded?" (An addition to the Town Hall? Not enough room, and on down the other possibilities.) "Our Choice: The Candle Factory. What Does It Offer?" (A library within a year and a half; central location; serves present and future needs.) "What Will the Project Cost?" (.69¢ per $41,000 property evaluation the first year; .23¢ the tenth year.)

A second sheet included the Position Paper of the Library Building Committee. It explained that "The Library Building Committee has spent seven years in a thorough search for a site for a new library for the town, and has decided that the Candle Factory building would be the best location." The advantages of the chosen site were enumerated, and the sheet went on to explain how the property could be purchased and how a Building Fund needed to be established to set aside money for renovation and furnishing of the new site.

Later, on the Saturday before the voting on the following
Monday, a sheet was handed out at public locations. It said
simply, "Vote *YES* on Question 1. The voters at Town
Meeting overwhelmingly approved acquiring and remodeling
the 'Candle Factory' for a new library. A *Yes* vote on *Question
1* will allow the Town to finance the project. Polls are open
Monday, May 5 from noon to 7 pm."

Town Meeting Vote

The composition of a town meeting has much to do with
the outcome of the votes. Votes can be influenced by older
people who are respected and speak to an issue, young
working couples with children vote one way, money-
conscious retirees vote another, cantankerous know-it-alls get
their say. On top of this, the selectmen and the Finance
Committee were focused on the cost. These two latter groups
were the biggest potential thorns at the meeting. "We weren't
sure if they were going to speak out against it," McIlroy said.
"You forget the agony of going through something like this.
It wasn't a unanimous decision from those two bodies. But at
the town meeting that often doesn't matter. It's the people
who make the decisions."

So she spoke to the people. "Last year the Police and Fire
Departments combined reported a total of 8,416 activities
requiring their involvement," she told the assembled people.
"The Library reported a circulation of 57,370 items, each of
those activities requiring staff involvement. The Shellfish
Department reported a harvest and landing of 50,436 bushels
at a value of $1,517,000. What is the value of the 57,170
interactions at the library when they included story hours for
three- and four-year-olds who will develop a lifelong love of
books and the ability to read and have access to all the books
they might need? What is the value when the staff helps a
student find the materials they need and they come back a
week or two later and happily announce they got an 'A' on
their paper or report? What is the value when the library can
make a difference between an 'A' and a 'C' or 'D'? What is the
value when the library helps to match you with a tutor who
can teach you to read? It is not as easy to measure as the value

of an oyster, but it is every bit as precious. For serving so many, so well, the library is a very economical department. Last year's budget for protection of persons and property was $915,000, public works $400,000, schools $1,084,000, library $75,000. You have spent virtually nothing on a library building for over 95 years. Once the major expenditure for a good, new library is made, the library will continue to run as an economical department. It does not have repeated large expenses like many other departments. This is not a criticism of any other department, simply a statement of fact."

The vote to acquire the property was 284 for, 11 against. The second vote for the renovation money was unanimous because the dissenters saw the will of the meeting and they didn't feel that strongly.

McIlroy emphasized that it is important to bring large sums of money from the taxpayers down to equivalents, such as "For the cost of a newspaper for a week you're buying yourself a new library." Statistics like these were very powerful, she said. "Get figures down to what people can understand. One young guy who didn't want to spend any money on a town library was at my presentation at the town meeting. I said that the town had spent nothing on a library building for 95 years; we were in the town hall. He said, 'Well, 95 years, that's a long time. Maybe it's about time.' You have to come up with statistics that are true but that can zing with meaning."

More Voting

In Massachusetts, Proposition 2½ means that a town cannot raise taxes each year by more than 2½ percent. This says that a big project such as a new library building cannot be paid for within the scope of Proposition 2½. An exemption has to be made on big capital projects so that taxes can be raised beyond the 2½ percent mark.

The library project needed a two-thirds majority vote at the town meeting. However, the exemption vote required a simple majority at the polls later—"which was a real scary deal," McIlroy said, "because all the people who sit in the woods and don't come to town meeting can do nothing but

then vote yes or no. That vote was much closer." It passed,
but only after further educating work by the library volunteers.

More Funding

Most projects begin by asking money for an architectural
study and from this get schematic drawings. Maybe at this
time the project goes to bid and gets a price. Then the library
committee comes in and asks for the amount of money from
the taxpayers. "We didn't do it that way," McIlroy said. "We
asked for the negotiated price of the land and a very informal
renovation cost, which turned out to be way off. Two years
later when we finally got to the bid stage, we had to go back
to town meeting for more money. It didn't turn people off
because Massachusetts was going through that incredible
boom when everybody had more work than they could
handle and construction costs had gone way up. Maybe, but
who knows, the proper way to do it would be to buy the land
and appropriate the money for the architecturals, and then
the next year come back with the model and working
drawings, with the exact cost to show the town. Actually, it
was an incredible leap of faith the town took for us, but in our
situation we knew we had to act. The land was here, and we
were asking the people to pay half a million dollars."
    Yet the library didn't lose support for proceeding back-
wards, "which shows what a good library means to people in
a small town. We're a very user-oriented library."
    It turned out that another $700,000 was needed to finish
the renovation. Meanwhile, the Funding Committee of volunteers raised $180,000 on its own, good for a small town.
The committee raised the money while at the same time
generating interest in community projects. Artists gave of
their talent, and residents attended town-centered events. For
instance, 200 people at $10 a person attended a harvest buffet
at the Wellfleet Oyster House for the benefit of the library.
More than 300 people attended a summer reading, at $10 a
person, that featured Marge Piercy, Annie Dillard and Mary
Gordon on stage. Noam Chomsky spoke for the benefit of

the library, and Javier Gonzales, a local artist, gave a print that was auctioned off, raising $20,000. A quilt was raffled off.

Two years later this money was subtracted from what the Building Committee needed to ask the town for—an additional half million dollars. "In essence," McIlroy said, "we needed another $700,000, but we were able to say we raised, at that point, $150,000."

In the end, Wellfleet now has a Public Library that is spacious, well-lighted, welcoming, up-to-date, well stocked, and well run. No longer is it cramped, musty, uncomfortable, and unpleasant to work in. The new one has a large meeting room accommodating 100 people for cultural events and art exhibits, a large children's section, ample work space, quiet study areas, a sound and video studio, a kitchen, a periodical section, plus a feeling of brightness and energy. The years of work and anxiety paid off, and much of the success is credited to keeping people informed and predisposed to appreciating the important contribution a library provides them. "There are always the same reasons for having to build a library," McIlroy said, "and perhaps some people say it better than others. But you do have to put it out to the public."

7   Computer Changeover

As a concept, computers are no longer revolutionary, high-tech exotica. People see the work of computers in banks, markets, and automobiles during their everyday lives. Ordinary people are familiar with them in general, have definite opinions about their usefulness, blame them for mistakes on their utility bills, and fear them for the intrusive power of historical detail that computers accumulate with such facility about their past. So the general public is more or less used to the presence of computers in one form or another.

When a library changes its paper system to an electronic one, however, library patrons often grow alarmed. Usually, the alarm stems from the sudden shock of encountering a computerized library system without due warning or sufficient preparation. While computers can be of immeasurable help to library staff, their chief value should be to improve service to library users. This in part means preparing patrons for the changeover as well as providing continuing aid and information when computer systems are expanded.

Brochures and Flyers

One of the most effective ways of communicating basic information is by way of inexpensive brochures and flyers. They are easy to stack in public view for distribution from the circulation desk or a table at the main entrance. They can be either picked up by the patron or given as something concrete to take away from a librarian who has answered a question or explained a concept about computers. Have plenty of them, but any one-sheeter or stapled 20-pager should be attractively printed, which is easy today with desktop (computer) publishing.

Whatever the format, the information should be basic and crystal clear. Presume that your public is not deeply immersed in computer science. All terms should be unequivocably defined, no matter how obvious they may be to you. An accessible definition educates those who do not understand, as well as reinforces those who do. A "menu" may be logical as an extension of the ordinary meaning of the word, but for people confronting a computer system for the first time, the word in an unfamiliar context may seem more complicated than it is. So define just about every key word—menu, online, database, file, modem, and the rest.

The Dartmouth College Library in Hanover, New Hampshire, for example, distributes a clear explanation of how to use its general catalog computer system. The 10 × 12-inch flyer is printed on good stock, designed without flourishes or gimmicks, and is folded vertically in three. Basic questions are asked and answered: "What Is An Online Search? An online search is electronic access to information sources or databases using a microcomputer or terminal. These databases may be located a considerable distance from Hanover and contain information drawn from one or more of the following sources: journals, magazines, books, indexes, abstracts," and so forth through eighteen more possibilities.

The questions and answers continue in the same light—simple and easy to comprehend. "Why Request an Online Search?" "How Is the Online Search Done?" "What Do You Get from an Online Search?" "What Is the Cost of an Online Search?" "Location of Search Services and Consulting Services."

Other similar material is readily available about the computer system on campus. Special collections, such as the Dana Biomedical Library, have their own brochures specifying what is available, hours of service, telephone number. One flyer lists all the "minicourses" on how to use the computer systems—the complete Online Catalog—DARTMED, CANCERLIT, and others. The flyer alleviates the inevitable questions from patrons: "For all courses: no registration, no cost, no pre-requisites, no exams."

Another flyer in attention-getting type states: "Grateful Med. In only 30 minutes of your time you can learn what it is and see it in action at the Dana Biomedical Library." Dates for these demonstrations are listed, and the tone of the flyer is welcoming.

For those who don't like to use computers in order to learn about computers, a 24-page, 8½ × 11-inch "Users' Guide to the Online Catalog" at Dartmouth is divided into 11 sections that explain the step-by-step process of a computer search and how to print your results. The brochure guide is stapled and punched with three holes for placing in a binder for later reference.

A sense of conveying genuine, pleasant service to anyone interested in making use of the library system easier and more complete is as important to a flyer as is the content. If this tone does not show, the content will be ignored and your effort lost.

Behind the Computer Scenes

Educating a library staff about computers well before the public use of them in your library instills confidence in the staff, which in turn instills confidence in patrons. This conveys a sense of efficiency in the overall operation of your library.

Changing a stamp-and-card circulation system to a computerized one offers a double opportunity if your staff is involved in the switch. First, you get the changeover done cheaper, and, secondly, the staff gets the feel of computers and understands how they work, what they can do and not do.

The Peterborough (N.H.) Town Library, for example, decided to switch to a computer circulation system and have its staff and volunteer Friends of the Library directly involved in the changeover. The best part of the changeover, Director Ann Geisel said, was that the staff had access to the computer in the back room long before the public ever saw it. For eighteen months staff members, including herself, typed in data for two hours a day several days a week. The work of data input done in-house was less expensive than hiring outside help and also provided hand-on experience for staff members. Time-consuming and tedious the work was, sometimes just sitting at the computer and typing in the title/author information, but the long-time project, by simple osmosis, produced a basic working knowledge of computers that staff members would not otherwise have.

This particular circulation system was an IBM clone hardware system with Data Trek software, which is a circulation package programmed specifically for libraries. At the time Geisel decided on this system, few companies were catering to small libraries, although more sophisticated software was available for large libraries (the Peterborough Library was designed for 3,000 patrons in a 5,000-population town). Altogether the hardware and software cost $5,000, relatively inexpensive and a good price for a circulation system for this size library.

Peterborough, the first tax-supported library in the world, was the first library in New Hampshire to buy the program. Since then all Strategic Air Command libraries in the United States, the Ohio Penal System, branch libraries of the Boston Public Library, and many others in New Hampshire and elsewhere now use it.

Private Preparation

At the same time that the Peterborough Town Library staff members were transferring card catalog data into the computer behind the scenes, other staff members were talking now and then about the computer-to-come to the patrons. Meanwhile, two volunteer members of the Friends of the Library worked on inserting bar codes in all the books and other circulating materials.

Geisel seized the public relations opportunity. She didn't wait until all the work was done to make use of publicity for the library. She mentioned the data inputting and bar coding from time to time in her weekly newspaper column. Then a separate article and photo of the volunteers bar coding were printed in the paper. This kept the notion of computer transfer in front of the public eye before the actual change-over went into public operation. By publicizing this early, Geisel kept the public informed and thereby eased the transition to a computer circulation system, and also took advantage of a legitimate news event in progress to maintain her overall public relations program. Waiting until the new system went into effect would have increased the tension such a changeover creates, not to mention losing a chance to place the library into view.

Public Preparation

Prior to computerizing the circulation system of the Peterborough Library, Geisel concentrated her annual reports for two years on the coming library automation. These joined the steady stream of news releases and general talk of the changeover to prepare the public for the switch.

Then, prior to the big day the library held a well-advertised, in-house blitz to re-register all patrons with bar codes on their new library cards. Notices were tacked on the bulletin board at the library entrance, catchy flyers were put out for distribution at the circulation desk, and every time patrons checked out books new cards were substituted for old ones.

Geisel then closed the library for two days (after ample warning signs on the entrance doors and in news releases). These two days focused on a staff workshop covering all the problems that might crop up with the inauguration of the new system. Closing the library to train the staff for contingencies held better promise of a smooth transition than having the staff fumble from scratch about problems while patrons waited in line at the checkout desk. All possible configurations that the staff might face at the front desk were confronted first behind closed doors—from how to renew material and process overdues to checking out books and magazines. This further helped ease the transition for both staff and patrons.

Pay Off

Geisel credits the smooth transition of the Peterborough Library to a computerized circulation system to informing the public beforehand and training the staff in the back room and during closed hours. Few problems occurred because of this. In retrospect, she took a lesson from the good acceptance of a new building program several years earlier when the public knew what would happen well before the ground breaking and interruptive construction. She figured that informing patrons again long before the actual new circulation system went into operation would help in the same way.

Once in operation, the computer system generated only a few negative comments, most of them stemming from the printout that accompanied every transaction at the desk; the printout contains all materials due and is a large sheet of paper to deal with. After people said, "Oh, all those trees," now the circulation clerks offer the patron a choice of whether to take a printout or not.

The other negative reaction was, "I hope you're not going to computerize the catalog." Patrons know that this is the next step, and many don't like the notion. After all, patrons don't have to touch a computer for circulation, but they do for catalog use. When the library does look to the computerization of the catalog, Geisel knows what to do and is prepared, with past experience, to keep the public well informed of progress as the library moves to the inevitable.

University Programs

Computer-assisted instruction (CAI) at the college and university levels, and at the higher grades of some high schools, is increasing. As more card catalogs are changed to online computer catalogs, so is a fresh approach needed to orientate students to effective use of computers in libraries. Using computers to orientate students to the basics of libraries has a number of advantages, including freeing librarians for more advanced instruction in bibliographic searches and accommodating the scheduling of crowded days for both students and staff. Not only are librarians relieved by computers from the formidable task of teaching hundreds, and sometimes thousands, of new students each fall, but the instruction can be a direct, personal experience for students, which offers the opportunity for better learning.

The emphasis here is to underscore the importance of

appealing to students in your programs, to keep their interest high and acute. One way is to use video to spark interest. You can create your own with scenes and personnel that are familiar to students, or you can purchase a ready-made video instruction tape. New York University Libraries, for instance, offer a 10-minute color video called "Cover All Bases," a tape of library skills depicted with a storyline using baseball analogies. With humor and baseball terms, the video explains how to use reference works, bibliographies, periodical indexes, and other resources. The tape is available for purchase. A video is an accessible way of introducing students to your library, and can be a useful preamble to a direct, computer-assisted instruction program.

The Mansfield University Program

The Library Department of Mansfield University in Mansfield, Pa. was in the vanguard of computer-assisted instruction (CAI) for library skills. Under Larry Nesbit, director of the department, the college library already had a vigorous public services program, so when Deanna Nipp, a Science Librarians, suggested developing a CAI program, the idea found a welcome. On a sabbatical she created the program directly for the campus library and the annual influx of new students. The CAI program went into operation in the spring of 1983, and has been effective for both staff and students over the years.

Titled "Search and . . . Find It!" the program is written to show students how their library functions and is organized, how the Library of Congress call number system works and where to find the call numbers in the building, how to use the *Readers' Guide to Periodical Literature,* how to find books and journals, where and what other library services are available beyond the Main Library. It tells what reference librarians do and how the circulation department works. It shows what the elements of a citation are and how these elements are applied to indexes.

Mansfield University, a state campus with 3,000 students in a 4,000-population borough, has a 206,000-book volume library with 2,233 current periodicals, besides microfilm and microvolumes. The library supports the programs for 68 undergraduate programs and eight masters' degree programs. Approximately 800-900 students enter the university each year, and applying a microcomputer to help teach them the basics of the campus libraries has turned out well.

Nipp developed the computer program to relieve professional librarians for more advanced resource instruction, but equal emphasis was put on the fact that little appropriate software was available, and certainly none that specifically interpreted the Mansfield Libraries.

Priscilla Older, Social and Behavioral Science Librarian and Coordinator of Bibliographic Instruction, recently revised the program. This was necessary because the library was going to an online catalog (the card catalog is closed) and several indexes are now on the computer. "The program provides an orientation to the library and instructs students in the fundamentals of searching," she said. "It's deliberately kept very simple."

Using a modern tool—a computer—catches the attention of students. But some students have never used one. In effect, they're learning two subjects: how to use a computer and how to use a library. Even inserting a disk into a computer and removing it aren't that simple if you've never done it before, which is why the computer instructions to the student are in unequivocal, informal style.

Some students have a fear of libraries that stems from bad past experiences. To give them something impersonal like a computer program can be unsettling. "What we try to do and emphasize, and it's repeated many times in the program," Older said, "is for students to consult a reference librarian if they have any questions."

What the Students Do

Using the program is voluntary, not a Mansfield University requirement. However, two-thirds of all students use the program. When students wish to use the program, they pick up a notebook with a disk in it at the circulation desk. The instructions treat the students as if they have never used a computer before. They take the disk back to the computer lab in the library; the library has terminals around the campus but the library staff has arranged to use only these library terminals in case students have questions; they are close by so that reference librarians can be asked questions, as the program repeatedly advises.

The program is in game format. At the conclusion points are totalled. Then two printouts are made, one for the students to take and one for the library to file for four years. The program sometimes takes students two hours, others half this, depending on their sophistication with libraries. The average is about one hour and 20 minutes.

The Program

"Search and . . . Find It!" is subtitled "A Game of Orientation to the Mansfield University Libraries." All the computer screen instructions avoid any computerese or techolingua goofiness. The instructions are in plain language, such as "Press C to continue." Reassurances are scattered throughout—"If you are unfamiliar with using computers and feel some anxiety about whether you'll know which button to push, you can relax. The game will always tell you."

Nine games are included. They include "Where to go for help," "Call numbers used in the MU Libraries," "Locating a book in the Main Library," "Finding a Magazine." Each step of the game is designed to show a logical progression in finding out information or locating a book, periodical, or index. Nothing is presumed, an axiom of good public relations.

After the students complete the program, they shut off the computer (instructions are in the blue notebook), return the disk to the circulation desk, and get the printed results.

Does It Work?

The program has been pre- and post-tested for learning. Some slight improvement in learning library skills is evident. "But the main thing," Older said of most of the first-generation college students of Mansfield, "is that the students say they like it." She emphasizes also that this program is merely the first step in student instruction in the use of a library. Other programs include more focused bibliographic instruction by librarians teaching directly in classrooms. Further instruction includes advanced strategy in using computers, other book and online indexing, and orientation to indexes specializing in advanced student fields.

A major advantage of computer-assisted instruction is the cost effectiveness. Before "Search and . . . Find It!" the library department sponsored orientation program classes and took most of the freshmen entering the university. Four librarians taught classes of 500 students in batches of 30. This was tedious for both students and librarians, and absorbed much professional time. The new program was very much more effective in terms of librarians' time and energy, and students learned better. In addition, students can run through the computer program at any time the library is open, including doing only half the program at a time.

Older says that "Search and . . . Find It!" could also be applied to public and school libraries. Information about adapting the program to other libraries, at virtually no cost, is available by writing to the Main Library, Mansfield University, Mansfield, PA 16933.

Service First

Technological whizbangs glitter with toy-like temptations. Librarians can slip easily into the seductive mechanics and marvels of our modern age, but the thrills of toys in tuxedos aren't what libraries are all about. In the end they aren't the ends. They are, however, sometimes wonderful means to fulfill one of our major goals—to refresh and enlighten the human spirit.

8   Newspapers

By the tradition of the printed word, newspapers are singularly related to libraries. However, this shared tradition should not be taken for granted. It must be understood and nurtured for the most productive result.

Article I

Probably the most important bond between newspapers and libraries is Article I of the Bill of Rights:

> Congress shall make no law respecting an establishment of religion, or prohibiting the free exercise thereof; or abridging the freedom of speech, or of the press; or the right of the people peaceably to assemble, and to petition the Government for a redress of grievances.

Freedom of the press and intellectual freedom are the primordial thrusts of both newspapers and libraries. Without them newspapers and libraries may provide us with entertainment, but they certainly won't give us the information we need in a self-governing nation. Freedom of speech for an individual is a vital social strength, but freedom of the press to write, print, and distribute a breadth of news and opinions from nongovernment sources that may be read by many people and referred to later is the fulcrum of a truly free society. Article I does not guarantee the freedom to print the *truth,* for who will determine what this truth is? It is the meandering trail toward truth that it guarantees, not the truth itself. This colossal freedom seeds the philosophical rationale for both newspapers and libraries and gives them a stature that cannot be casually ignored.

Honor Article I. And use it to advantage. Let it be known

that both newspapers and libraries provide news and entertainment, that they both guarantee a wide range of opinions and judgments, that their combined heritages are vital to the healthy cerebral climate of a people. The existence of yellow journalism may be quickly raised by those who disagree with this view, as may the Fiske Report about the lack of intellectual guts of some California librarians. Nevertheless, the bond between newspapers and librarians is real and, more likely than not, local editors will bend over backwards to support you, the local librarian—if you earn their support.

Know the Editor

The first step toward earning this support is to know the editor. Do you know his or her name right now? Even in this day of overnight express mail, telephones, fax machines, and television, nothing beats personal contact. Maybe the phonovision will suffice in the future, but, as it is now, a professional business visit to a newspaper office is the best way to pave the bumpy road for your publicity releases. As always, personal contact is still one of the most important factors in getting jobs done for you by someone else.

Know the Paper

Read your target newspaper with more than passing interest. See whether or not the paper shies away from controversial issues, such as sex-education books on the open shelf. See if the paper has a certain intellectual, literary undercurrent or whether the general trend is toward straight hard-core news. This may give you a clue about whether to submit releases that emphasize programs involving issues or programs of events.

Remember that no two newspapers are alike in tempo and tenor. Some papers are superficial in their news reporting, some highly involved with in-depth coverage. Some are fat with advertising, some thin. Some are careless with copy while others demand top-grade writing. The dailies generally extend their horizons to the regional, national, and international scenes, while the weeklies generally cover only the local items of interest. The large metropolitan newspapers as the *New York Times,* the *Washington Post,* or the *Los Angeles Times* are extraordinarily complex operations that involve a legion of personnel on the editorial floor alone. On the other hand, small-town papers may have only two or three staff members, who handle the reporting, writing, editing, headlining, and sometimes the make-up and printing. Newspapers may be exciting places to work or watch work, but policies and procedures are seldom alike from one to another.

The functional success of newspapers in this country is an indication that newspapermen and women by and large accomplish their goals competently. That is, newspapers cull and disseminate the description of events that have importance and interest to the people of a community. The paid circulation of daily newspapers in the United States now reaches beyond 63 million. Daily papers number 1,642; weeklies, monthlies, and other papers total 10,457—far from a dwindling supply. The number of existing dailies is not as impressive as the 2,600 that were published in 1910, but the strong ones that remain are better papers, staffed by better-trained personnel, and have a more mature sense of responsibility. It is said that newspapers took two hundred years to establish a freedom from undue government harassment and interference with editorial policy, and only fifty years to work with the responsibility that accompanies this freedom.

Too Little Time and Space

Still, despite the varying sizes, shapes, and policies of the many newspapers all over this diverse country, fundamental similarities do exist among newspaper offices. The first is that there is never, absolutely never, enough time in the day or space in the paper to include all the news that could be, should be, and is fit to print. Everyday notable events are not included on the dummy sheets because time does not permit investigation, writing, and editing of the story by the available personnel. Everyday notable events are not included because the physical format of the newspaper itself does not permit the inclusion of all stories. Both these limitations of time and space are largely governed by economics.

Influencing Editors

The other similarity is that all newspapers are run by people. And people may be influenced. They may be persuaded by you to allow some of this precious time and space for your needs. Editors are not omniscient. They cannot be expected to know the needs of libraries simply because these needs exist. Editors must be told, they must read it somewhere, they must be made aware of situations.

The importance of knowing editors, then, cannot be overemphasized. The larger the paper, the more editors there are—city editors, managing editors, lifestyle editors, sports editors, feature editors, state, national, and wire editors. The large dailies have assistants in these slots as well. Whatever your local situation, getting acquainted with editors is valuable for your library in the long run. Some editors are difficult to approach, some impossible. Whenever the occasion arises, however, invite the ones you think might come to a special talk at the library or to a controversial panel discussion. If an editor is at a party, be sure to talk with him or her, introduce yourself, start talking libraries. If you can't get to an editor personally, send in background information that may be useful to the paper. Don't be shy. An editor is always looking for ideas for a paper as much as you should be searching for ways to promote your library. Help an editor any way you can. Perhaps a local scandal is in full swing. Look up some pertinent background information that an editor might use. Send it to the paper. It may provide an editor with some leads and it may give you some notice.

Study the Paper

Simply knowing an editor doesn't mean your releases will be printed, however. Knowing an editor's name is useful and will usually help you get past the receptionist. It will not be a library publicity panacea. A newspaper editor is a professional, and professionals like to work with other professionals. Editors like to work with people who know something about what the newspaper field attempts to accomplish, more than such fundamentals as that the ads support the paper and that you may buy it on the street corner.

Know some of the newspaper jargon. You're a librarian, and you can find out about some of the common newspaper terms in your reference books (or at the end of this chapter) before you meet an editor. It'll be easier on both of you if the editor won't have to stop and explain the trade terms every few moments. After awhile the editor will realize you have an interest in the newspaper field, that you understand some of the problems, appreciate what the paper tries to accomplish. Some of your interest in an editor's field may rub off into the editor's becoming interested in yours.

Prepare for the Unexpected

Most library news releases don't involve spot news events that rise to a quick head and require immediate reporting. Such events as fires, robberies, spontaneous press conferences, riots, and other hard-core news must be structured into the daily paper as quickly as possible. On the other hand, a speaker on community race relations at the local public library is usually planned well in advance. Special exhibits or arrival of special acquisitions leave plenty of time available to draw up a release and submit it to an editor with one or two or more days leeway.

Occasionally the unexpected happens. Someone breaks into the library at night and escapes with your only copy of the Gutenberg Bible. Or a self-appointed censor suddenly harangues the City Council about how certain books in your library are ravaging the minds of the youth in the community. Or one of the local alcoholics in town writes a letter to the editor to castigate the libertine policies of the library that ignore the sweet smell of marijuana in the back stacks of the young adult section.

Your good relations with an editor may now produce results. For the good of the library it is often best to react quickly to instances such as the above. A statement from the librarian in the next issue of the newspaper could squelch many problems that might otherwise grow larger. By working with an editor on other tamer issues and by instilling a sense of your reliability and accuracy, and of what you as a librarian are trying to do for the community, you already have the door open. The editor may not agree with your side of the story, but the theft of a Gutenberg Bible, censorship, and public charges of running a pot mill are news items. The editor knows from past experience to expect a reasonable statement from you to balance and explain other facts in the story.

The Deadline

From your side of it, you already have found out one of the most important elements of the newspaper world: the deadline, the time of day when all copy must be across an editor's desk in order to be printed in the next issue, if at all. You asked the editor long ago what the deadlines were. You typed them out and filed them away for quick retrieval.

You see the letter to the editor in the afternoon paper about marijuana smoking in your young adult section. You decide that a library is a place of action and you're going to let everyone know it. You check the editor's deadline and call up. "I know you have a 12:30 deadline tomorrow," you say. "How 'bout if I write up an answer to that letter today and have it to you in plenty of time for tomorrow's paper?"

"Fair enough," the editor says, knowing you'll come through. Besides, you'll spice up the letters section. "I'll hold space for about 150 words."

"I'll bring it down myself at 11:00."

Be Reliable

You do bring the letter on time because you said you would. This is important to newspaper editors. It's also important that the paper be read. You've helped the editor and the editor has helped you. The public library must be a reliable place.

This reliability you've established for yourself will carry over into your news releases. The next time the editor sees a release with your name on it he or she will be more likely to pay the little extra special attention that could easily help persuade that the item has merit and is worthy of printing. By now the editor is assured that your material is accurate, imaginative, journalistically appropriate, and professional.

News Articles

Generally newspapers use two types of stories: the straight news article and the feature article. The news story must answer these questions about an event:

Who	When
What	Why
Where	How

A one-paragraph summary with the answers to these questions begins nearly all news articles, long or short. This is the basic newspaper principle of the inverted-pyramid style. The broadest view of an event is reported in the lead paragraph of the story. As the article progresses the scope is gradually narrowed to more and more particulars and details. This structure of a news story allows an editor to eliminate from the bottom of the story as much as is needed to fit the story into the space left on the page. By structuring a story so that it can be cut from the bottom instead of requiring a complete rewrite, an editor may get on with the job as easily and quickly as possible. The inverted-pyramid style gives an editor the necessary option of cutting a ten-paragraph article to three or four and still have it make intelligible reading.

Feature Stories

On the other hand, a feature story is structured with more unity and balance. The end of many feature stories cannot really be cut without destroying the completeness of the article. The end of the article sometimes refers meaningfully to the beginning. In addition, the feature story appears to be more casual and informal in its writing and to express more of a point of view.

Whereas a news article reports an event as straightforwardly and objectively as possible, a feature story is designed to arouse interest and insight into the meaning and possibilities of everyday life. Librarians may use both forms effectively in publicity releases.

Here is an example of a news story:

ALASKA LIBRARY ASSOCIATION

RELEASE DATE: March 3, 19—	FOR INFORMATION: (Your name, address, and phone number)

PULITZER-WINNER HARKEY TO SPEAK
AT LIBRARY ASSOCIATION BANQUET

Ira Harkey, Pulitzer prize-winning journalist, will be featured speaker at the banquet of the annual conference of the Alaska Library Association in Fairbanks, March 10–11, Paul McCarthy, president of the Association, announced.

Harkey, now visiting journalism professor at the University of Alaska, won the Pulitzer prize in editorial writing in 1963 for his courageous stand on integration in Mississippi.

"We are delighted that Mr. Harkey will speak at the conference banquet," McCarthy said. "Librarians have a special allegiance to the intellectual freedom he defended as editor of his paper."

Harkey published the *Pascagoula Chronicle* in Mississippi for 14 years and turned the paper from a weekly into a daily. He achieved national recognition when he stood up to Mississippi Governor Ross Barnett and the Ku Klux Klan.

His book *The Smell of Burning Crosses* tells the story of the pressures and threats he went through as editor. It was published in 1967 and is now in its fourth printing.

Harkey's talk will cap an intensive conference study of the recent survey conducted by the Public Administration Service of library service throughout Alaska.

Proposals for improving and extending library facilities
and service will be discussed in light of legislation and
creative innovations.

-30-

This straight news release is set in the standard format used
by nearly all organizations and companies. The letterhead is
usually in color, easy to read, and, most of all, uniquely
identifiable. Some releases are printed on soft-colored paper as
one more trick to stop an editor's eye. This is not necessary and
is, in fact, thought to be amateurish by some professionals.

If for some reason you wish the release to be printed only
on or after a certain date, the standard format in the upper-left
corner is: "RELEASE DATE: March 3, 19–." Otherwise, it is
in this form: "FOR IMMEDIATE RELEASE."

Include Your Name and Number

All releases sent to newspapers should have a name,
address, and telephone number in case an editor needs
clarification of some kind or wishes the story to be expanded.
An editor may question a quote or a statistic and want to
verify it quickly. If no name and number are available on the
release, rather than using the release after a quick call an
editor may forget about it because it is too much trouble and
too time-consuming to track down a number through other
channels. It happens.

The Head

Make it easy for editors to use a news release. The two-line
headline at the top of the release is designed to give an editor
a quick idea of what the story is about. The actual head may or
may not be used in the paper. This doesn't matter. What
matters is that the head on the release should provoke an
interest to read the rest of the release. If it does, then chances
are better that the story will be printed.

So the heading should capsulize the content of the release
with as much thoroughness and importance as possible.
Normally two-line heads are designed so that the first line

may be read as an entity without absolutely requiring that the second be read. Try to avoid ending any line of a head with a preposition. They're weak.

The Content

The first paragraph of a simple story should include all the essential names, places, and dates. The lead paragraph should be thought of as a complete story in itself, in case for any reason it might be cut to this one paragraph. The rest of the story enlarges on the lead, fills in background, adds specifics. Quoting someone involved in the story or some authority related to the core of the story adds a dimension of human interest. As a matter of style, quotes break up the article for easier reading. Besides, people are always interested in what other people have to say.

The end of the story in a news release should be indicated either by several dashes in the center of the page, XXX's, or by the symbol -30-. The "thirty" is the traditional ending to a newspaper story and is often used.

Look carefully at the news release about Ira Harkey. The importance of each paragraph to the overall intent of the article diminishes as the story progresses down the page. An editor may easily cut the bottom paragraph without hurting the story. In fact, the release could be cut in half if this were the only space available, and still the article would tell its story in a comprehensive way. This inverted-pyramid style provides an editor with great flexibility.

A feature story, however, is written differently, but the same release format may be used:

WOODHILL PUBLIC LIBRARY

FOR IMMEDIATE   FOR INFORMATION:
RELEASE   (Your name, address,
                                      and phone number)

LIBRARY SURVEY REVEALS CHANGE IN READING TASTES

Sons and daughters are not reading the simple, innocent stories they used to—but neither are their parents.

A recent survey by librarians at the Woodhill Public Library shows that the known change in reading tastes has changed far more drastically than expected, Mr. William Davis, head librarian, reported.

"Young people are reading more and more books about social situations, child abuse, and race relations," Davis said. "Not long ago sports, romance, and adventure books were the favorites."

Young people have become involved in social questions either directly or through their older brothers and sisters who are in the Peace Corps, VISTA, or other volunteer work.

Book publishing reflects this trend, Davis said.

"Even adult reading tastes have changed a great deal," Davis said of the survey. "Science fiction, nonfiction dealing with deep social problems, history, and political science books are beginning to seriously challenge the popular mystery and how-to-do-it shelves."

The survey, conducted over a two-month period at the circulation desk, also shows that more adults are reading more "adult" novels.

Light escape novels are still popular, but fiction dealing with intimate situations of love and marriage is growing in circulation.

Davis said the survey was made in order to show librarians how best to serve the people of the community.

It also showed that mothers and fathers reflect the changes in current situations just as their sons and daughters do.

-30-

A critical look at this feature story shows that nearly all the paragraphs are interrelated. The difficulty of cutting too many of the paragraphs without undermining the unity of the story tends to force the printing of the article in its entirety. The end of the story can't be cut casually without damaging the lead references to both young people and adults. The story unfolds as it progresses rather than narrowing in importance as a straight news story does.

This may be either good or bad. An editor may not have room for an entire feature story and may set the article aside and never use it. If it is used, the library gains a better display in the newspaper than it would with a smaller three-paragraph news article that has been cut from eight.

Release Forms

Some newspapers send outline forms to publicity directors of clubs and organizations, libraries included. These forms have lines available for the name of your library, date of meetings, where held, the agenda, names of guest speakers, topic and brief content of the talk, and any other information you wish to add. From these forms a reporter will write the article. However, if it is at all feasible, write your own stories in news-release form. This gives you a greater degree of control over what you want to say and how you want to say it. The article may not come out in the paper in the identical way you submitted the release, but at least you have made it easier for an editor and have provided material that may be changed according to his or her style and taste.

News, Not Publicity

The most vital point to remember is that an editor could not care less about giving your library publicity. An editor is interested in giving readers news. This is the job. This is the reason for *news*papers—to publish a paper that contains articles of timely and human interest.

True, the correct format of a news release is an indication to an editor that you know something about the newspaper game. And true, the structure of your news story testifies that you understand the audience you're writing for. Yet in the end these are accoutrements of news releases, more important than the distinctive letterhead and the -30- at the end of the story, but still accoutrements.

Never forget that the substance of a release is the value of the content, nothing more, nothing less. Does the release say something? Is it a report of a significant change of events, of potential interest to a segment of the newspaper's readership? Does the story have meaning and relevance beyond the people directly involved in the story? In other words, does the story have a purpose over and above that of getting the name of the library into print?

Remember that an editor is interested in what has changed or could be reported as changed in the world in the last twenty-four hours for a daily, the last week for a weekly. News is change. Change, however, is not necessarily news. From a librarian's point of view the changes that have extramural meaning are the ones that have to be selected and promoted.

Write to Communicate

The releases must be crisp, imaginative, and important. No one has found a substitute for the simple declarative sentence. Respect it. Write short sentences. Write short paragraphs. Be direct. Simplify, simplify. Your object is not to get into print but to communicate.

Rudolf Flesch, in *The Art of Readable Writing,* reminds us that the Elizabethan written sentence averaged about forty-five words, the Victorian sentence twenty-nine words. The average written sentence today is about twenty words and falling. So write short, simple, direct, declarative sentences. Write them as if you were perked up at full steam ahead, especially your lead paragraph. Research in newspaper readership indicates that lively writing may increase readership of an article by up to 75 percent. News releases from your library need this crisp writing. The average man reads only about 20 percent of a big-city paper, a woman, only 16 percent.

Photographs

Because of the odds that librarians face in gaining reader attention, news releases need as much support as possible. The best support is a good photograph. Editors know that a photo accompanying a story gives this story, at the minimum, a 50-percent better chance of being read.

With this in mind, you should include a photo with a news release from your library whenever possible. Even if your releases and photos aren't used every time, the minimal expense will be far outweighed by a maximum readership when one of your pictures does get printed. Most larger libraries now own a quality camera, usually a 35mm. Even if you have to use your own camera, the expense of film, development, and printing of one or two enlargements is worth the effort.

Often a newspaper itself will send a photographer and reporter to develop a story. This depends on the significance of the idea you submit to an editor.

Here are some of the important items to remember when you take your own photos and offer them to newspapers. First of all, have your photo tell a story. Don't let it appear posed, like having Father's hand on Mother's shoulder. Portraits and mugshots are usually dull. Avoid them. Try instead to freeze an action of some kind, whether it's children's faces entranced in a story hour or a researching professor oblivious to the outside world.

Whatever the shot, keep it simple. Good newspaper photos tell a single uncomplicated story. Think in terms of symbolizing the article. Let the article provide the details. Let the photo abstract the main idea of the article. Keep the background of the photo uncluttered, the main subject centered and full-blown. Limit group shots to two and three individuals, if possible. The larger the groups the less attractive the picture in print. Be daring in your camera angles and subjects. Be artful, not arty. An editor wants imaginative pictures, but clear and straightforward.

Despite the printing of some color photos, nearly all newspapers want 8″ × 10″ black-and-white glossy prints from non-staff sources. Each print should be captioned with the identity of all the principal individuals, what they're doing in the picture and where. A photo accompanying an article should support the article. The two work together, not separately. People in a photo should be mentioned in the article. The caption on the photo should be typed and taped either on the back of the print or folded down at the bottom. This latter way an editor may read the caption and look at the photo at the same time. Protect the photo from bending and creasing by placing it between two pieces of cardboard in an envelope.

A good photograph of your library in action is extremely valuable. It may often mean the difference between getting an article in a newspaper or not, especially if an editor is short on artwork for the day. Once it's in the paper, a good photo may also attract the most attention from the general reader.

Glossary

Ad	An advertisement
Add	Additional material written for a story already or partially completed
Advance	A story about a forthcoming event, such as a dedication or speech
Angle	Viewpoint that is emphasized in a story
AP	Associated Press, one of the major international news syndicates
Art	Any photograph, chart, or drawing used to illustrate an article
Beat	Any special office or agency a reporter is assigned in order to gather news regularly, such as the police beat
By-line	Name of writer of any news or feature story, as "By Davey Jones"
Caption	Written description of any artwork
City Editor	Assigns and edits all news of local events
Copy	Any written material
Deadline	Time when articles are due on the editor's desk; varies according to paper

Dummy	A computer-drawn sketch for placing stories physically on a page
Editorialize	To represent opinions and value judgments in ill-disguised news stories
Follow-up	A story that includes results or new details of a previous story
Glossy	A very shiny photographic print needed for reproduction in halftones
Handout	Any publicity release, usually unsolicited
Head	A headline
Human Interest	Stories that appeal very personally or emotionally
Kill	To stop writing or printing a story
Layout	Placing photographs, other artwork, and copy in aesthetic arrangement
Lead	Opening of any story, normally but not necessarily limited to the first paragraph
Localize	To slant or emphasize the story for local community interest
Lower Case	Small letters
"More"	Used at bottom of a page when the story continues onto another page
Morgue	The newspaper's library
Obit	An obituary
Pad	To enlarge an article without enlarging the substance

Pics	Pictures, photographs
Play	Prominence given a story either by space or headline
Query	Memo or letter asking if an editor is interested in seeing a particular story
Release	News or feature story mailed to any editor by a nonstaff source
Scoop	Exclusive story, usually of importance; not now used much by reporters
Sidebar	Short article of interest related to the main story
Slant	Angle or emphasis to a story
Stringer	Usually part-time, nonstaff supplier of news items or ideas; paid by the published column inch
Style	Particular rules of grammar, spelling, numbering, and other methods of writing
-30-	Indication of the end of a story; XXX or ### or the writer's initials are also used to end a story
UPI	United Press International, one of the major international news syndicates

9 Radio and Television

The Federal Communications Commission is charged with the responsibility to regulate radio- and television-station procedures, techniques, and programming in the United States. The FCC grants or renews broadcasting licenses to radio and television stations throughout the country. The three key factors that govern the FCC in granting broadcasting licenses are "public interest, convenience, and necessity."

Public-Interest Programming

Of the three, public interest has been confirmed time and again as the fundamental responsibility of broadcasting stations. Court decisions, congressional hearings, and federal laws over the decades have established "public interest" as the principal guideline by which radio and television stations are evaluated and by which the public grants them permission to use the public air waves.

Normally the FCC does not question a particular program. This would involve censorship and possibly lead to dangerous prior restraint of individual shows. The Commission, however, does review the past program schedules of stations, and, on the basis of a balanced programming that includes obvious efforts toward serving the public interest, grants individual stations licenses or renewals. Application forms for licenses to broadcast require a station to detail the amount of air time devoted to entertainment, religion, agriculture, news discussion, speeches, education, and miscellaneous programs. An analysis of these applications and in-field investigations provides FCC officials with an indication of whether a station is serving merely its own interests or those of the public.

Some stations are not granted licenses as a result of

inadequate programming in the public interest. One classic example of the refusal of the FCC to grant a license, in this case to a radio station operated by a medical doctor, was based upon the doctor's prescription of medical help through letters only. This was considered "inimical to the public health, and safety, and for that reason is not in the public interest." Other stations have been denied licenses because of a lack of local live talent or because they broadcast too few educational programs. Promotion of lotteries and use of obscene language are expressly stipulated by law as reasons for denial or broadcast licensing. Enforcement of laws, however, is a different question and is influenced by the political appointment of FCC commissioners.

Educational Program Needs

FCC regulation of the air waves is based not merely upon negative principles of restraint; it also takes into account positive promotion of public-interest programming. Traditionally the two types of programs the FCC has always favored most as serving the primary interests of the public are religious and educational programs. This emphasis of the FCC continues to the present.

Librarians couldn't ask for much more:

- The law promotes public-interest programming.

- The FCC favors educational programs.

- The library is the nearest thing to an all-encompassing educational institution.

- Broadcasting stations by law must devote time to public-interest programs.

- Station managers are constantly looking for local talent and imaginative programming to satisfy public-interest requirements.

- Public-interest time is available.

• The time must go to somebody.

• Why shouldn't the time go to librarians?

The FCC states explicitly that broadcasting stations must "serve the needs and purposes of nonprofit organizations such as educational institutions." Libraries are nonprofit educational organizations of the highest order and as such may promote their purposes without paying commercial fees for advertising their wares. Under normal circumstances air time for libraries is free.

Fortunately, librarians may taken advantage of the powerful media of radio and television to spread the good tidings of libraries without having to pay expensive commercial rates. To be sure, the spot announcements or five-minute messages or half-hour programs about libraries need to be imaginative, competent, and reliable, but this is what librarians are supposed to be anyway.

Here are some hints on how to take advantage of this largely untouched broadcasting bonanza:

RADIO

Radio is far from being superseded by television. On the contrary, contemporary radio is a vibrant social force. Literally hundreds of millions of radios are turned on in homes and automobiles.

Limited Only by Imagination

Radio is clearly a medium of mass communication that librarians should be using more extensively. In the first place, radio is not only relatively easy to use, it is highly effective as well. It is limited only by imagination. Time and place have no limits in radio. Unlike television or newspapers, radio gives the writer virtually absolute control over what the listener receives as the message. The writer is the one who selects what will be heard and therefore imagined, felt, and understood in the listener's mind.

In using radio, librarians must be aware that it is an informal medium of communication. The message and voice must reflect a casual tone, as if the voice were speaking to one person. The stilted, formal language used by public speakers when they address an auditorium full of people has no place on radio. This approach quickly turns off the listener. The key to successful radio is to remember at all times—from idea-and-planning stage to writing and production of the script—that the broadcasting microphone is a medium of warmth, of friendly, direct, personal, imaginative connection to listeners.

Sound Is All

Everything that radio conveys is accomplished through sound or the lack of sound. Music, sound effects, pauses, and especially narration or dialogue form the basis of radio. Words, of course, are the primary ingredients.

Just as librarians should know the basics of submitting a news release to a newspaper by typing it in double space, so should they know how many words are delivered how fast by the average radio announcer:

10 seconds	25 words
20 seconds	45 words
30 seconds	65 words
45 seconds	100 words
1 minute	125 words
1½ minutes	190 words
2 minutes	250 words

This scale is approximate. Many radio announcers speak faster than indicated here, others slower, depending upon the station, the personality of the announcer, the inflexions and hesitations, the complexity of ideas. Still, the scale may be used as a general guide.

Station-Break Announcements

All radio stations are required by law to have what are commonly known as station breaks. This is the time a station identifies itself to the listening public: "This is your music station, KPOL, Los Angeles," or "Keep listenin' to the discs we're spinnin' here at station WHKL, Langston," or "Your news station of the Northwest, Station KWRT, Yakutat." They are all familiar to radio listeners on the hour and half-hour.

These standard but frequent station breaks offer librarians opportunities to cash in on livening up a standard radio format. Station program managers are always on the lookout for something new: a gimmick, a catchy phrase, a fresh idea. Radio uses material as fast as the second hand sweeps around the clock. New material is constantly in demand to keep a radio station interesting to the listening public.

One way to do this might be to present a station manager with a series of short twenty-second identification breaks plugging your library.

Here's all you do:

ID STATION BREAK
(20 seconds)

This is station KJOP in ＿＿＿＿＿＿ where the public library recently received a boxful of best-sellers, including ＿＿＿＿＿, ＿＿＿＿＿, ＿＿＿＿＿, and ＿＿＿＿＿. The Public Library has books, phonograph records, newspapers, magazines, and other library material available for adults and children alike. Visit it soon.

This form painlessly eases the way from one message right into the next. If you listen closely, you'll recognize this format in many instances. You'll hear these spot announcements for many other nonprofit organizations, such as the March of Dimes, and for nationally celebrated weeks, such as Raisin Week. Libraries are not heard as often, probably because librarians haven't taken sufficient advantage of the available time, as other professionals have.

Weather Announcements

The same format may be used following other standard fare on radio, such as the weather forecast:

WEATHER FORECAST
(30 seconds)

So it looks like rain for the next few days. It might be a good time to check in at the _____ Public Library and check out a couple of good books to read. The library is located at _____ and _____ Streets and has everything from mysteries and science fiction to books on sports, fishing, and home improvements. It's open from 9 o'clock in the morning until 10 o'clock each weeknight, except Saturday, when it closes at 6 o'clock in the evening. Convenient enough? Then why don't you read some of that rainy weather away?

With a little imagination and some twist of words, other systems besides the public library may be given notice. The general public may be informed that school, university, and special libraries are serving their own particular clienteles, too.

Library Dramas

Librarians should make the most of whatever medium they use. The free-spinning wheels of imagination run wild in radio and should be exploited to the fullest, especially in dramatic form. Nothing stirs a listener like a good story, and radio uses a story as no other medium. A few highly selective words, a few sound effects, and a few stings of music quickly grab a listener's attention and unleash the wonderment and magnetism of an unfolding drama.

The following is an example both of the basic radio script format and of a one-minute story that could possibly be used for library promotion on radio:

MUSIC	ESTABLISHING THEME (SUCH AS THE FIRST FOUR NOTES OF BEETHOVEN'S FIFTH SYMPHONY).
NARRATOR	It wasn't too long ago that a brilliant biologist discovered the secret of creating life.

SOUND   BOILING WATER IN TEST TUBE.

NARRATOR   But he couldn't stop there. He haunted butcher shops and dissecting rooms through the city in the stealth of night . . .

SOUND   OWL HOOTING, CAT SCREECH-ING.

NARRATOR   . . . until at last he collected enough raw materials to fashion an eight-foot monster. He endowed the monster with life, enough life for the monster to rise from the platform and walk among men.

SOUND   HEAVY FOOTSTEPS, HEAVY BREATHING.

NARRATOR   The monster was grotesque and frightened all who saw him. He escaped to the country and sought strangers as friends.

SOUND   KNOCK ON DOOR. DOOR OPENS.

NARRATOR   But whoever saw him was terrified.

SOUND   SHORT, QUICK GASP. DOOR SLAMS.

NARRATOR   The forlorn monster demanded that the scientist create a mate to his own likeness for him to love as a companion. But the scientist refused for fear a whole new race of monsters would result. The monster became enraged.

SOUND   TERRIFYING CRY OF RAGE. TEST TUBES ARE SMASHED ON THE LABORATORY FLOOR.

NARRATOR	He escaped the scientist again and began to kill men and women at random in his hatred for mankind. He killed young children and he strangled the scientist's young bride. He terrified the entire countryside until finally . . .
MUSIC	THEME.
NARRATOR	You can find out what happened next in the novel *Frankenstein,* by Mary Wollstonecraft Shelley, by checking it out at the _____ Library. The library has thousands of fascinating books. Visit it soon.

This is no way to end a story, but the buildup to the climax only to have it remain unresolved should be enough to drive anybody to the library.

Don't worry about sound effects. Nearly any effect you might want is on one of the scores of sound effects records nearly every radio station has in its record library.

The staff of the Richards Library in Newport, New Hampshire, produced its own radio spot announcements with rewarding listener results. A local station broadcast each for one week. Some of the mini-dramas were based on humorous incidents in the library, such as the following:

LIBRARIAN	Hi there!
STUDENT	Hi. (*shyly*)
LIBRARIAN	Can I help you find something?
STUDENT	Well, maybe.
LIBRARIAN	Did you have something special in mind?
STUDENT	Well, yes—I have to read a book.

LIBRARIAN	Do you want a particular book?
STUDENT	Yes, I have to have something on Louisiana Apricot.
LIBRARIAN	I don't understand—you want a book on the state of Louisiana?
STUDENT	No—Louisiana Apricot.
LIBRARIAN	Is that the state tree of Louisiana?
STUDENT	No, I need Louisiana Apricot.
LIBRARIAN	Are you referring to a particular author—the person who wrote the book?
STUDENT	Yeah, I need a book by her.
LIBRARIAN	Do you mean Louisa May Alcott?
STUDENT	Yeah, that's the one—you got anything by her?
ANNOUNCER	Students can find the answers at the public library, whether they are looking for Louisa May Alcott or the state of Louisiana. This message is brought to you by the Richard Library of Newport and radio station WCNL.

Book Reviews

Some librarians feel more comfortable producing short book reviews for radio. A book review is standard fare, expected from librarians by the general public. Such reviews may be somewhat difficult to sell to a station manager, but then again, they may be just what the station needs. All you can do is ask, and all a station manager can say is yes or no.

The library may be promoted on radio by many ways and

means besides book reviews. If you're not ready for high drama, then by all means try the book review. What matters is to get the name of the library into the public consciousness.

A radio review should be just this—a review and not a critique. Your review should aim to encourage the reading of a particular book and should not be filled with heavy reasons why the listener shouldn't read it. Leave this to the literary critics. On radio your review should be somewhat light and airy. It should be written to be heard, not to be read from a printed page. Choose words for conversation rather than for a lecture or an essay. If you are given a regular time slot by the program manager of the station, identifying yourself might help build up a following for the library. Be sure to tagline the end of your review with a note that the particular book you just reviewed may be borrowed from your library.

Here are some hints to include in your review:

- Mention the title of the book two or three times throughout your review.

- Quote two or three lines directly from the book.

- Include particulars, such as names, dates, and places; avoid flowery generalizations.

- If nonfiction, try to pick a book that touches a listener's daily life, such as books on money, health, family life, self-improvement.

- Use the second person, "you," to make the review tailored directly to the listener.

Keep in mind that reviewing a book should be designed not merely to encourage the reading of this particular book but to encourage reading and use of the library in general. The following is a sample review for a two-and-a-half-minute book review for radio:

RADIO REVIEW
(2 minutes, 30 seconds)

Morton Mintz's book called *By Prescription Only* may be increasing the sales of Excedrin—because Excedrin headache number 57 is finding out that the control of the manufacture and sales of pills and drugs is not what you think it is.

By Prescription Only may shatter some of the illusions you have about the Food and Drug Administration, the American Medical Association, and the drug manufacturers in this country. Evidently, the apparent irresponsibility of all these institutions in promoting and releasing drugs to consumers—us—is none too slight.

Before 1938 no drug of any kind had to be shown to be either safe or effective. At that time the Food and Drug Administration was finally authorized to require a drug to be shown to be at least safe. Not until October, 1964, were drugs required to be shown to be safe *and* effective.

This last legislation resulted largely from the exhaustive investigation of the Kefauver-Harris Senate Subcommittee on Antitrust and Monopoly, a hearing on physician ownership of drugstores and drug companies.

Mintz writes in his book *By Prescription Only* that—quote—"The Kefauver Hearings, which spanned two and one-half years, established beyond doubt that useless drugs were being wantonly marketed and prescribed, with resultant extensive death and injury." Unquote.

Since 1965, Mintz writes, the American Medical Association has been repeatedly exposed as a leading purveyor of false or misleading drug advertisements to its more than quarter-million members. This, in addition to the vast inventiveness of the drug industry, has outpaced the Food and Drug Administration's capacity for control of the American Way of Drugging.

Between 1938 and 1960 an average of 375 new drug products a year cleared the Food and Drug Administration, many of them with irresponsible, superficial testing. The real laboratory ended up being your own body.

For example, success stories of a drug called Norlestrin, a Parke, David Co. oral contraceptive, were placed in newspapers before the Food and Drug Administration approval. This and other examples, together with the American Medical Association's evident lack of interest in the safety of specific drugs, create a dangerous situation for consumers, especially those who have been conditioned by articles in such magazines as

McCall's and *Ladies' Home Journal* to believe that new
drugs are automatically better drugs.

Morton Mintz may be crying in the desert with his
book, but he does so with the conviction, evidence, and
effectiveness of Ralph Nader's book *Unsafe at Any Speed*
for safer automobiles and Rachel Carson's book *The
Silent Spring* for responsible use of pesticides.

You may borrow a copy of *By Prescription Only* by
Morton Mintz at your _____ Library.

The advantage of writing your own reviews is that you can
fashion the review of certain books to your own particular
community. Listeners distinguish a locally produced program
quite readily from a nationally produced one. If you do it
yourself, a local announcer may introduce the review with
something along the lines of: "And now a quick look at a
recent book from Oscar Oswalt of our own _____
Library."

Endless Possibilities

The sky is the limit in the use librarians may make of radio.
Short spot announcements about your library may be effective over a long-range plan. With some work and refreshing
ideas, librarians should be able to get public-service time for
half-hour programs or possibly even hour programs, depending upon the city and station.

The library is a fulcrum of ideas in a community. In what
better position, then, could a library be to sponsor a debate on
a current controversy? Perhaps as a public service a library
could sponsor a panel on a hot issue that is before the City
Council, or on the value of an alternative press or the
evolution of the modern novel. A library could tape-record a
talk by a prominent speaker and then, under the sponsorship
of the library, present it to the radio station for broadcasting.
Perhaps a library could sponsor a weekly or daily question-
and-answer program in which listeners write in requests for
information on any subject they choose.

The list of possibilities for radio programs for the benefit of
the community and your library is virtually endless. Such

programs do take time and do take work. Yet any design for
library promotion cannot afford to overlook, nor fail to use,
this inexpensive but effective means of mass communication
that librarians have too long ignored.

TELEVISION

Through satellites television has indeed transformed the
earth into a global village in which major events, such as the
landing on the moon, have world participation at the moment
the events are happening. The involvement and emotional
power resulting from television have yet to be fully defined
by experts.

Television has changed the world just as it has changed the
modern psyche. It is considered not only the biggest industrial
growth in the history of the United States but also the biggest
cultural growth. The invasion of the television set into the
consciousness of modern Americans has radically changed
social, economic, and educational structures. To what direction
is another question. The fact is that today students are said to
learn more outside the classroom than inside, much of the
learning coming directly from television. The National Citizens
Committee for Broadcasting estimates that the average American child spends 22,000 hours in front of a TV screen before
age eighteen. A child receives "50 percent more of his basic
education and initial impressions in front of a television set than
in the classroom," the Committee reports.

These few figures only serve notice to librarians that the
modern miracle of television is an extraordinarily impressive
part of our society. Librarians must be aware of it, and know
how to use it. Here's how:

You may approach television in two basic ways. Either ask
the program director or news editor to send a taping crew to
your library or produce a show yourself for broadcast over the
station.

Prepare for TV Crews

If you feel you have a rather special event at your library
and your local television station news director agrees, don't

merely hang up the telephone and wait for the camera crew to come to the library. Prepare for them. Arrange an appropriate area for an interview. Be sure plenty of space is available for the crew to set up lights and move around for various camera angles.

Have some coffee brewing for them. Keep pencils and paper handy. Be glad to see them. Greet them with a smile. After all, they don't have to come out and they aren't bound by law to report your event favorably.

Fact Sheet

Present a reporter with a brief, clear, single-page fact sheet about your event. Plan ahead. Think what you want to tell the public about the event. Jot down notes. Anticipate a reporter's questions. The questions may be elementary in order to inform the layperson, but such questions are sometimes the most difficult to answer.

Visual Movement

Prepare for action. Visual movement is the central ingredient of television. Plan some movement for your interview, any kind of movement, but don't limit the action to your mouth.

Suppose your special event is a highly successful display of popular books that were once banned by law, books such as *The Adventures of Tom Sawyer, The Last Temptation of Christ,* or *Robin Hood.* You might prepare a simple chart with large letters listing some of the books and the states or countries in which they were outlawed. This is all you need on the chart. Anything else is confusing and too jumbled for a TV screen.

Place the books nearby so that you may pick them up as you talk to the reporter and camera. Have patrons or staff members available so that the camera may record people browsing through the exhibit. Display a copy of an old newspaper headline that states one of the books was banned.

With preparation an interview may be fast-paced, interesting, and convincing. A camera can videotape these displays and later in editing the final product cut back and forth to these scenes while the reporter is talking with you. The actual interview will probably be quite short; television reporting usually is. Nevertheless, you will win friends at the television station by doing your best to help the crew present a feature item of significance and human interest for the public on the evening news.

Your Own Productions

Single news reports that a TV crew tapes at your library are relatively easy to prepare. A program or a series that you produce on your own requires more involvement. Modern, portable, three-quarter inch, broadcast-quality videotape cameras make your own productions easier to accomplish. The cameras are fully automatic. Borrowing or renting camera, electronic editing equipment, and closed-circuit transmission sets opens up intriguing public relations possibilities, such as orientation and special-subject series. Although the projection quality is usually lower, television projects using videotape are much like filming, only easier.

First of all, knowing some of the unique features of television is necessary. When planning a television production, keep in mind the medium itself. A TV screen is not a cinemascope wall in a 1,500-seat auditorium, but a modest sized set in a lighted living room that competes with noise from children in the back room. What appears on the screen is perforce restricted to small, uncluttered, sensibly simple scenes.

Keep It Simple

Large groups, large sets, and large plots are clumsy on a tiny TV set. Large ideas are workable, but they, too, must be diluted to eliminate detailed complexity. So plan your library panel show or interview or instructional television class with as few stars as possible, with sets that are utterly simple and uncluttered, with a clear, forward sequence and logic, and with ideas that are couched in terms and neatness acceptable for a mass audience. Bear in mind that your audience cannot question you or ask that you repeat an idea that was not clear to them.

Television is a visual medium primarily, and to be successful in exploiting its full potential you must have many objects to show as your production progresses. These objects may be charts, books, film clips, still photographs, covers of phonograph records, other people, or anything or anybody of relevance that moves the camera about or changes scenes.

Television combines sight and sound and may be highly effective in manipulating these two features. Pictures and commentary don't necessarily need to be synchronized in context. For example, you may show a videotape clip that illustrates the frantic inner workings of a beehive on the screen while at the same time running voice comment about a recent book on the sociological studies of mass transmit systems in the country. The resultant effect would be far more gripping than showing a standard subway scene in New York City.

Close-Ups

Another important feature of television is the use of close-up camera shots. Be sure close-ups are scattered throughout your production—close-ups of people's reactions to questions, of signs, book titles, letters, signatures, special displays, and so forth. Television is an intimate medium by the mere fact that it enters the home. To bring the home viewers closer to your production, simply bring them closer to the people and objects that you use. Always write an ample supply of close shots into your script. They provide you with a tool to show your audience many facts and figures, actions and reactions, objects and subjects, without constantly talking about them at the same time.

Script Format

The format of a television script varies from the Hollywood-type film script shown in Chapter 10 to the standard TV script shown below. The two-column format stems from the days of live television production, when the synchronization of video and audio action was critical: the style of the script had to show the simultaneous actions as clearly as possible.

The following excerpt is taken from a script used in the production of a class for instructional television shown in upper elementary classrooms. Notice the many changes of scenes to keep the screen action moving:

VIDEO	*AUDIO*
SUPER TITLES (Things Go Better with Books)	
MCU (Medium Close-Up) on host	Hi! Welcome to our series on the library. As you know, the library is a special place. It's where the action is . . . if you know how to find it. And that's why I'm here—to show some of the fascinating things you can find in the library and how to find them quickly and easily. You know the library is your library . . . it's just for you. Whether you want to find information for your studies or just a good book to read—the library has what you want. Come with me and let's visit some school libraries.
SLIDES OF SCHOOL LI-BRARIES	TAPE OF CHILDREN'S OPINIONS ABOUT THEIR LIBRARIES
MCU ON HOST	There are so many books in your library. You can find information about practically anything you can think of, from aardvarks to wombats and from mythology to the Alamo. All the books are

organized in a special way—this
is true of all libraries. There are
certain sections devoted to different kinds of books.

DOLLY OUT TO INCLUDE
BIOGRAPHIES ON TABLE

Let's take the books about famous persons—biographies. All
the biographies are together and
are arranged alphabetically by
the last name of the famous
person about whom the book
was written.

SUPER 92-BIOGRAPHY

Each biography is marked with
92 on the spine. These biographies here include stories about
several famous persons. Here's a
biography about John F. Kennedy, the president. The spine
marking is 92. The title, *The
Living JFK*. The author, Robert
N. Webb.

CU ON COVER OF BOOK

TAPE OF JFK MAKING
SPEECH

FADE TO PIC OF JFK

FADE TO SECOND PIC

FADE TO THIRD PIC

MCU ON HOST

There are biographies in your
library about so many famous
men and women. Here's one on
Sacajawea, the Shoshone Indian
girl who acted as guide and in-
terpreter for the famous Lewis
and Clark expedition.

CU ON COVER OF BOOK

TAPE OF SACAJAWEA
WORDS

FADE TO SILHOUETTE OF
SACAJAWEA

MCU ON HOST

Check your library for an exciting true story of your favorite famous person.

FLIP OF BIOG SECTION

Remember—all the biographies—the books about famous persons—are together in one area of your library. This section will be marked 92-Biography.

FLIP OF BIOG ARRANGE-MENT

Biographies are arranged alphabetically by the famous person's last name. If you want to read the life story of Daniel Boone, start looking at the beginning of the Biography section. For the exciting adventures of the Wright brothers, check the end of the section.

MCU ON HOST

Biographies are part of the nonfiction section in the library. Your school library and your public library use the Dewey Decimal Classification System to place all nonfiction books on the same subject together on the shelves.

DOLLY OUT TO INCLUDE MYTHOLOGY BOOKS. SU-PER 292-MYTHOLOGY

For example, all books on Greek mythology are at 292. Here are some of the books on Greek mythology you might find in your library.

MCU ON HOST

We can take another example . . . books on science experiments. Most of these will be found at 507.2.

SUPER 507.2-SCIENCE EX-PERIMENTS

Do you know where the nonfiction section is in your library? Remember . . . on the spine of each nonfiction book you'll find

	a number. This number can tell you what the book is about and where to locate the book.
FLIP ON NONFICTION	All nonfiction books are arranged on the shelf numerically—from the smallest number to the largest.
MCU ON HOST	Now let's think for a minute of favorite make-believe stories. We call them fiction books and they can be found in the fiction section. And there are so many kinds of books to be found there. . . .
FLIP OF HORSES (slowly pan 3 covers, 25 seconds)	TAPE OF HORSE MUSIC AS CAMERA PANS BOOK COVERS
FLIP OF MYSTERY (pan 3 covers, 25 seconds)	TAPE OF MYSTERY MUSIC
FLIP OF SCIENCE FICTION (pan 3 covers, 25 seconds)	TAPE OF SCIENCE FICTION MUSIC

Fit Visuals to Screen

In preparing such a script with charts and diagrams, maintain a consistency of lettering and size of your materials. Fit your visuals to the proportions of the home-viewing television screen. This makes your presentation as aesthetically pleasing as possible.

The dimensions of the TV screen are in the ratio of three to four. This means that for every three units of height there are four corresponding units of width. Your one-dimensional visuals should be in the same proportion—three to four. They should also be surrounded with sufficient white borders to allow for the maladjustment of the vertical and horizontal dials of individual home sets. This way the edges of your visuals are not cut off on the home set but are still centered on the screen in the same ratio as the screen itself.

Nearly all television stations are equipped to project 35mm and 16mm moving film, plus transparent black-and-white or color slides on the screen. Most stations can also handle the projection of photographic prints, newspaper clippings, maps, and other such materials that can be shown through a specially equipped and specially mounted opaque projector. The standard flip card for letters and numbers is still used, although electronic lettering is replacing it. These cards are stacked unfastened on an easel and then yanked singly out of sight to reveal the next card.

Choosing Clothes for TV

When you're to present yourself in front of a TV camera, dress simply. Choose colors in the middle of the spectrum: avoid whites and blacks, even today with color television. Men should avoid white dress shirts, women should stay away from black dresses. The sparkle of jewelry usually drives technicians up the wall, and the explosion of light from sequins drives them completely out of their minds. Avoid both.

Keep Calm, Cool, and Collected

When on camera, move easily and without panic, no matter what happens behind the scenes. Keep calm and keep smiling. When you're on stage alone, look directly into the camera or at least in the general direction. Try to prevent your eyes from wandering about the studio. Don't try to cover up your mistakes by pretending nothing happened. Simply say, "Oh, I'm sorry. I meant to say. . . ." Thinking, planning, and rehearsing will eliminate most of your mistakes beforehand, but if they do occur, just be natural. Acknowledge them. Nothing is more refreshing and engaging.

Idiot Sheets

Virtually all the highest-paid performers on television have cue cards or idiot sheets of their script to guide them while they are on camera. Don't be embarrassed to do the same. If use of the electronic prompters can't be arranged, write your script in large, clear printing on long strips of white butcher paper. Someone in the studio will hold them beside the cameras while you're speaking to help you in case you forget what comes next. Some performers have the entire script written out word for word, others merely need key words.

Photos and News Releases

If you prefer to bypass this type of programming alto-gether, other outlets are available to promote your library on television. One simple way is to submit a news release and a photograph or two to the news director of your location station. A photograph should not be the same one you submit to a newspaper. A newspaper editor prefers an 8″ × 10″ black-and-white glossy print. A television news director prefers the same size, but it should be a dull matte-finish color print on double-weight paper, or color transparencies.

A TV news release should be much shorter than a newspa-per release and should be styled in a terse, conversational format. The reading time should be typed at the top of the page and should be no longer than thirty seconds. Here's an example:

RELEASE DATE: FOR INFORMATION:
Immediately   (Your name and address)

READING TIME: 20 seconds
David Hanson, Director of the Galbraith Memorial Public Library, was awarded the John Cotton Dana Award last Friday for developing community interest in the library. The award was presented to Hanson at the annual convention of the American Library Association in Detroit. More than 8,000 librarians from around the country attended the convention.

Hanson was cited for his work in public relations programs. He has been Director of the Library since January, 1989.

Split-Second Timing

Television in the United States is a split-second operation. Program directors fill their schedules with timing down to the single second. Entertainment programs, commercials, special announcements, and station breaks must be produced according to certain specified time limits. Each segment of a day's programming must fit together so that the TV sets in living rooms of millions of homes have an image on it at all times.

To make the job easier for program directors and to predispose them toward using your tape rather than rejecting it, fit it into the standard time restrictions. Be accurate in stipulating how long your tape runs. Nothing is more irritating to a director than to have your tape too long or too short. Be precise if you want a second opportunity to submit another one.

The standard time slots for tapes on television are these:

10 seconds	9½ minutes
20 seconds	14½ minutes
1 minute	29½ minutes
4½ minutes	59½ minutes

Competition for television time is thick and furious. High commercial rates for time slots reflect both the demand and the effectiveness of television. The video dimension adds greatly to the preparation requirements for anything submitted to television. This must be considered carefully in any library promotion project in terms of local time, effort, and finances.

Worth the Effort

The extraordinary mileage gained from exposing your library programs on television to a wide audience warrants the adventure. Success may be measured either in getting a simple thirty-second news release and photograph of your crowded building on the air, or an elaborate thirteen-week library-produced panel show high on the Nielson ratings. The obstacles are far from overwhelming. Many other professionals ply their trade over the broadcasting air waves; librarians need not be the exception.

Successful television presentations do take considerable work and preparation. What is important to remember, however, is that the regulations of the Federal Communications Commission require radio and television stations to air programs and announcements that benefit the public over and above commercial interests. Libraries, as professionals, are imaginative, consistent, and reliable, and have the sole purpose of serving this same public. Their use of television should increase.

Glossary

Academy Leader	Film strip at beginning of reel with numbers 8 to 3 shown one second apart to cue projectionist
Ad lib	Any words of movements not specifically written in a script
AFTRA	American Federation of Television and Radio Artists
Anncr	Announcer
ASCAP	American Society of Composers, Authors, and Publishers
Aspect Ratio	Height and width of standard television screen: 3 × 4
Audio	Any sound or lack of sound in broadcasting
Balop	Opaque projector used for television broadcasting
Clip	Short piece of film inserted in television program

Control Room	Where broadcast directors and technicians regulate the programs
Credits	Names of persons both in front of and behind the scenes in a production
CU	Close-Up
Cue	Signal to start program action
Dead	Electronic equipment not operating
Director	Person responsible for all factors of a broadcast production
Dolly	To pull camera in or out of scene
ECU	Extreme Close-Up shot of television scene
Fade	*Radio:* decrease in sound volume. *Television:* fade to black or fade in to scene
Flip	Words or illustrations on heavy card stock used for close-ups on television
Floor Crew	General production crew
Floor Manager	Responsible for transferring director's cues to performers
I.D.	Identification of radio or television station
Idiot Sheet	Cheat sheet with script for performers
Lavaliere	Portable microphone worn around the neck of a performer
Log	Program schedule
MCU	Medium Close-Up

Mike	Microphone
NAB	National Association of Broadcasters
Pace	Tempo of the production
Remote	Radio or television broadcast anywhere outside a station building
SAG	Screen Actors Guild
Spot	Either a short commercial or public-service message, or a studio light with a narrow beam
Super	To superimpose one picture over another on television
Talent	Performers
T.D.	Technical Director
Telop	Opaque projector for television
Transcription	A recording for either radio or television
UHF	Ultra High Frequency, used for television channels over 13
VHF	Very High Frequency, used for channels 2 through 13
Video	Visual side of production
Videotape	Records both video and audio television broadcasts for transmission and preservation
VTR	Videotape recorder

10   Videos and Slides

Marshall McLuhan, the mass communications sage, once said, "The movies, like the book, is a ditto device." He maintained that books and movies share an important communication advantage. Movies are to dramatic representation what the book was to the manuscript. Movies make available to many people at many times and places messages that otherwise would be restricted by stage productions for a few people at few times and places.

Today videotape has replaced film for home movies and for the advanced amateur making a presentation about a business or agency—or, in this case, a library. Unlike film, videotape doesn't need to be sent to a developing lab; it can be replayed immediately to check for mistakes or the need to change angles or action. With automatic light-sensing and exposure metering, sound recording, and other simplified features, videotaping a production about your library becomes much easier than filming. A video, of course, can be replayed through television screens at any appropriate terminal or set, allowing for individual and small-group showings. Although the resolution quality of videotape is less than that of film, the advantages of making a video outweigh this factor.

Three-quarter-inch tape is the choice for broadcast quality, requiring top-grade, expensive camera recorders. This is probably beyond your needs and resources. Besides, one of the by-products of these broadcast-quality camcorders to cameras is the subsequent production of multiple copies of the tape for commercial distribution. (Smaller, low-quality tape loses resolution as the number of copies made from the original increases.)

On the other hand, you can make perfectly acceptable videotapes for replaying in your library with a good quality, low-cost (or low-rental) video camera that uses quarter-inch tape. Most likely you will not be making hundreds and thousands of multiple copies. New models and updated variations on video cameras appear constantly on the market and should be investigated.

As for the making of a video, most of the same principles of filming apply to taping. As a bonus, some new video cameras are very lightweight, have special-effects lens built in, immediate editing capability, quality microphones, instant replay viewing options, and many other features that film cameras do not.

VIDEO

One goal of promotion programs is to reach as many people as possible within a reasonable cost figure. For libraries, videotape is a good, contemporary method of achieving this. Making your own tape—rather than purchasing ready-made products—allows you to shoot scenes that include your own library as background and faces that are familiar. This relevancy in your tape makes your promotion more immediate and meaningful and therefore attractive to the people you wish to reach.

Advantages of Tape

The advantages of videotapes for promotion include:

- Combination of in-motion sight and sound as one of the most effective means of communication yet developed

- Versatility in showing outdoor and indoor scenes, close-up of people and objects, taking audiences to normally inaccessible places, time elapses and other unique features

Plan!

An important step in making your tape is the planning. The more planning and thinking about your tape before the actual shooting of it, the better will be the final product. The process of taping and editing will be easier in nearly direct ratio to the time spent on this planning.

Ask yourself these preliminary questions:

- What is the tape to accomplish? What aspect of the library most needs explaining?

- What must be shown to accomplish the goal of the tape?

- How many principal performers might be needed? Can you get them?

- What cannot be shown on this particular tape? What are the temporary features of the library?

- How long should the tape be and still remain appropriate to the subject?

- How long a life span do you want the tape to have?

- Should the tape have background music? What kind? Classical, piano, jazz, rock, dixieland, disco?

- How long should it take to shoot? Is there a deadline of some kind in order to preview it at a future special event?

- Outdoor and/or indoor scenes?

- Rent or borrow equipment? From whom? How much?

- What is the anticipated audience? Young people? Elders? Students?

- Who can help with the work? Who wants to help?

- Should it be a tape to give information primarily or one to promote an image primarily?

It is important to answer these and other questions relevant to your particular situation in concrete terms before doing anything else. Think ahead. Know your project inside and out. Know where you're going, how you're going to get there, and what you want the audience to learn specifically from your tape.

Don't rush it. Move step by step. Yes, definitely know the overall scope and mechanics of your tape, but move methodically down the line of the process.

Outline

At this stage of the planning a one-page outline in paragraph form is sufficient to present to others for discussion. One page is less heart-breaking to change than a fully detailed script. Whatever you do, be sure to put everything you've gathered about the videotape in writing in one notebook. So many cumulative details are involved in making a tape that the impossibility of remembering them all becomes quickly obvious.

Story Line

For maximum audience interest your script should have some elementary story line. In other words, have an internal reason why the camera moves about the library. A story line, no matter how rock-bottom basic, adds continuity to a tape and draws a viewer into the intended message. Pointing a camera at certain areas of a library is not enough. A story line also indicates to a viewer's subconscious that a videotape was structured, that it was indeed thought out with deliberation and not pieced together at random.

Say that your library has two floors. A simple but effective story line may be that the camera follows two patrons (students, parents, elders, researchers, or whomever) into the library to the card catalog. One patron finds what he wants in the subject catalog and goes to the first floor. The camera follows him and reveals to the audience what is available on the first floor.

Later, the camera picks up the second patron at the author-title catalog and follows her to the second floor, where she finds what she wants. In the process the camera points out to the audience what is available on the second floor of the library. Simple. Totally elementary. Yet enough to incorporate continuity and people-related interest in a ten- to fifteen-minute tape that might otherwise have been a helter-skelter strip of images.

Again—Plan, Plan, Plan!

Now talk to others about the proposed script. Bring up all the problems the script may entail. This is the time to do it. Plan, plan, plan. You know your library from the point of view of a librarian but not from making a video. Walk through the scenes as you see the script in your mind's eye. Ask these questions:

- Are electrical outlets conveniently available for the spotlight?

- What tables and chairs must be moved?

- At what time of day would it be best to shoot to avoid streaks of sunlight across the floor that might wreak havoc on light exposure?

- What calendars and clocks should be removed from the walls to eliminate dating?

- What camera angles at first glance seem feasible?

- Will the performers have enough room to move in front of the camera at the catalog, in the book stacks, at the microfilm table, in the periodical stacks?

Begin to think in terms of what the camera sees. Move about the scene with forefingers and thumbs in a square before the eye. This is how to isolate parts of the library as scenes the camera will record. Imagine what the camera will isolate as it photographs your script. Certain angles may eliminate unsightly dirty walls while others may include a beautiful painting on the wall to enhance the background of a scene. Think in terms of varying the scope of your angles. Walk through the library and think what might be shown in full-frame shots, medium shots, or close-ups. A performer walking to the front doors of the library might be a full shot, thumbing through the card catalog might be a medium shot, fingers on a particular card might be a close-up. The more you become the camera the better the final product.

The Talent

About some things you must be ruthless, and one of them is actors and actresses. Cooperative actors are definitely a must, especially when you're not paying them for their time and effort.

However, what ends up on the screen in front of your audience is not cooperation but people representing your library. So if you can find an all-American male who walks like he means it and an all-American female who smiles like she means it, you're on your way. Gathering your cast may not be easy, but whatever you do, consider your prospects carefully. Don't ask just anybody, because just anybody is not good enough for all your time, effort, and expense.

The Script

All this preliminary thinking about your video makes it easier for the next step—writing the script. One trick to ease the pain of visualizing the scenes in your mind is to draw the major scenes you plan. On one half of 5" × 7" cards draw outlines and stick figures of what you expect to shoot. On the second half of the cards write the stage directions, captions, or narration for this particular scene. Then number the cards to keep them in sequence. If you feel the need for more detailed planning, draw each and every scene you plan to tape. No rule says you can't do this. Some people find this method extremely helpful.

Once these cards are finished lay them out on a table or tack them to a board in the number sequence. This way you see the script as a whole and follow along almost as if it were the video itself; you can see at a glance—literally—how the general flow of the script appears. Perhaps you'll notice an abrupt break in continuity. Simply insert another card with a transition scene. This type of careful planning makes it far easier to repair a script beforehand than to truck out all the equipment and performers to shoot a needed scene that wasn't noticed during the first shooting schedule.

On the other hand, this storyboarding of your video gives you the opportunity to examine a script for any unnecessary scenes. Always keep in mind the essential goal of the video. Whatever is not absolutely essential to the script, yank out. This is another factor to be ruthless about. Do not include a scene of your actress taking a drink at the water fountain if it is not an important part of the script. Such a scene is unwanted and unnecessary. It wastes time and is a bore. Throw it out.

Another point to remember when constructing your script is that no scene is sacred. Any scene may be eliminated, changed, or added. What you create may be recreated. If a scene or narration doesn't fit, change it. At this point in the production a script is still arbitrary. Words may be changed or erased. Now is the time to do it.

You may use these story cards as your script, or translate them into a written script. Some people prefer to eliminate them altogether and go directly to a written script. Some people have enough imagination not to need to draw the scenes but head straight to the typewriter. The actual form of a script is not what matters. What matters is that there be a script. A script is absolutely essential. No two ways about it. Without a script to guide the production of a structured videotape, the worst headache in your last life will be nothing like the one ahead.

The more complete a script is, the smoother the actual shooting of the tape. Here's an excerpt of an actual script used for a university library. The form is that of a basic script used by motion picture and television productions:

TIGHT SHOT of Nancy as she passes through the entrance.

NARRATOR
. . . or Nancy, who is assigned a report on the life of Shakespeare for her English class . . .

TIGHT SHOT of Mark.

NARRATOR
. . . or Mark, who has to write a paper on super-conductivity for a science class.

INTERIOR SHOT as the two students enter the library doors. DIFFERENT ANGLE and PAN as they walk singly past the circulation desk to the card catalog; Nancy goes to the author-title catalog; Mark goes to the subject catalog.

NARRATOR

These students know that their library has more than 200,000 books and that the storage and retrieval of any of these 200,000 books may be an unnecessarily complex operation. But Nancy and Mark are familiar with some of the basic tools in their library.

REVERSE ANGLE of catalog area as the two students thumb through two catalog trays.

NARRATOR

This public card catalog is one of the most important keys to the books and materials in your library. It is a divided catalog, meaning that one section has books listed by subject only . . .

MEDIUM SHOT of subject catalog, including "subject" sign.

NARRATOR

. . . and the other section has books listed by both author and title only.

MEDIUM SHOT of author-title catalog, including "author/title" sign.
CLOSE SHOT of Nancy's hands as she thumbs through a tray and comes and stops at the author card she wants.
HOLD.

NARRATOR

This card gives Nancy the classification number for the book she wants. The number in the upper-left-hand corner is identical to the number on the spine of the book.

This particular script format makes the reading of camera angles, stage directions, words of narration, and general flow of the video easy to use in one tight package. On the average one page of single-space script runs between one and one-and-a-half minutes of screen time. This means that a good, tight fifteen-minute tape will have a written script of about ten to twelve pages.

Notice, too, that narration does not repeat in voice form what is communicated in visual form. Your own narrator should not say over the action of the video that "Nancy is coming through the front doors of the library to get a book from the library. First, she will go to the card catalog, thumb through the cards, and find the book she wants."

Keep in mind at all times that your tape will provide audiences with information in two fundamental forms—audio and visual. Other means of imparting information, such as music, tempo of the video, and camera angles, will be present in the tape, but your main concern at this point is what is spoken and what is seen. Don't confuse the two and don't overlap them unless it is absolutely necessary for clarity.

Taping the Script

After your script is completed and has been approved by the powers that be, you're ready for production. You have your actors and actresses, your equipment and tape. Fresh batteries are in the video camera and new lights in the spots. Enthusiasm is high. Cooperation supreme. You're ready to roll.

Here are some points to keep in mind as director, camera operator, writer, prompter, stage coach, mover-of-furniture:

If at all possible, shoot the script in straight sequence. Tape the first scene first, the second scene second, and so on down the line. By doing this you save immeasurable time and effort later when you're editing the unwanted exposed tape. In all probability you will have to shoot many scenes two or three times, maybe more, in order to get them as perfect as possible. Reshoot over the section of tape you do not want. If the entire script is on tape, scene by scene as it is written, cleaning up the final video will be far easier than if you have to cut out scene four from roll eight, scene eleven from roll three, scene seven from roll fourteen, and then rearrange them in proper sequence.

All scenes must be taped with a tripod. You want the actors to move, not the camera. A hand-held camera is more for newsreels and special effects in off-Hollywood pictures than for the type of video you've planned. The slightest camera movement is magnified many times on a screen. Use a tripod. It's a must for each and every scene.

Also, every roll of tape should be identified—although not every scene needs to be: you'll know the script intimately enough as you progress. However, borrow the traditional clapboard idea from the experts. Simply take a piece of paper and write a number on it. At the beginning of each new roll shoot a few seconds of its particular number. The number identifies this roll of tape on the tape itself. Then, for each scene on this roll, mark the number on the margin of the corresponding scene in the script. This indicates that the scene has already been shot and on which roll it is.

For example, mark *1* on a piece of paper. Have someone hold it in front of the camera and record it on the beginning of the first roll of tape you use. Then, with each scene on the script that is taped on this roll, mark *1* next to the scene in the script. This serves the dual purpose of reminding you what scenes have already been shot and also that these scenes are located on the number *1* roll. Be sure to mark *1* on the tape cartridge when you're finished with the roll. Of course, the best possible method for keeping track of the scenes and rolls of tape is still to shoot the script in straight sequence. Unfortunately, often this may be impossible for lack of performers at certain times, or because no sunlight is showing when you want it, or for other reasons. Keeping notes and written records of the progress of the taping is a good safeguard. It will be helpful during editing.

Have several copies of a script handy for marking and for other members of your crew to follow so that you don't miss anything. You're the director and therefore the boss of the entire production, but you can't remember everything. It's much easier to be reminded by someone else of a certain scene to shoot rather than to have to return the following day to set up the equipment and performers again.

The basic process of shooting each scene is this:

1) Determine camera angle.

2) Tell performers what the scene is all about and what you expect of them: how to walk, where to look, which directions to turn, what actions to perform.

3) Set up lights.

4) Walk the performers through the scene.

5) Walk the performers through the scene under the lights and follow them through the camera.

6) Tape the scene.

The Script as Guide

Normally each scene is created at the time of the taping. Angles may be changed from the script. Position of performers may be shifted. Remember that a script is merely a guide, not a gospel. Often what is in the mind's eye at the time of the writing of a script is not what is possible during the taping. Don't hesitate to veer away from a script if the realities don't fit the written word. Just follow a script as closely as possible, because each scene was written for an overall purpose and effect.

The Director

Undoubtedly you will shoot many scenes over again, especially when working with amateur performers. Keep the show moving. Encourage your actors and actresses. Give them specific direction. You know what you want, but they don't. Performers must be told what drawer to pull out, what angle to turn their shoulders, how to sit in their chairs, how fast to walk, what books to remove from the shelf, each and every particular. Be deliberate. Leave nothing to chance or ad lib. Everyone before and behind the camera will look to you for direction. This is the way it should be. One boss, and only one, must be present on the scene, and this is you, the director.

This doesn't mean you must be a tyrant, merely that you must be decisive and work to get the video made. Keep your cool. Work with the people. Be pleasant. Establish patterns of action and of pushing the production along. Keep thinking in terms of what the camera is recording. Remember that the jokes behind the camera will not be shown on the screen.

And for Dewey's sakes, have your actors and actresses look pleasant. Have them smile. Your library is not a mausoleum. It's a nice, comfortable place to visit. It's full of wonder. It's attractive and inviting, but it won't appear so to your viewers if your performers look perfunctory and heavy-eyed.

Lighting

One technical way to enliven a scene is to make it bright with good lighting, even with modern video cameras. Most indoor scenes require special made-to-order lighting. A minimum of two spotlights is essential. Three spots are better and four best. They may be used this way:

> *First spot*: 45-degree angle to the scene on the left side of the camera.

> *Second spot*: 45-degree angle on the right side of the camera.

> *Third spot*: either 45-degree angle downward from above the camera or directly to the side of the scene.

> *Fourth spot*: directly to the other side of the scene.

Main lights are called key lighting, secondary lights fill lighting. Try to maintain the same lighting intensity on the scenes throughout the script. This gives an even exposure to the scene and a consistency of color to the screening of the final video. Without more elaborate equipment this consistency of exposure is difficult to maintain, but do the best you can. You may need to have your crew members hand-carry the spots off-camera as they follow the performers through a scene. This type of production may be necessary to light the actors and actresses along dark corridors. Remember that people like to look at other people. So keep your performers well lighted and bright looking.

Stage the Performers Consistently

Try to keep your actors and actresses consistently staged. Unless you're an extraordinary cinematographic genius, the shooting of your script will run several days. Yet the final screening takes only about ten to fifteen minutes. This means that during the short screening of the finished product the actors and actresses must look the same, dress the same, and, in fact, be the same throughout the video.

Take notes of the stage scene before any coffee or lunch break and especially at the end of the day. Note what dresses or slacks the actors wore in the video, whether they wore short or long sleeves, in which hand they carried books, the positions of tables and chairs, who stood next to whom and at what angle. Notice which side of the head an actor's hair is brushed and be sure it is in the same style on the following day. Make certain your stars return to the scene with the same shoes, belts, briefcases. Details are extremely important. The final video of fifteen minutes magnifies any details out of joint. The result is only natural: if an actress has her hair style to the left in one scene and to the right in the following scene, the audience may find this amusing, amateurish, and annoying. More attention will be paid to the abrupt switch in hair styles than to what the actress is attempting to depict in a particular scene.

Action!

You're recording life in a library, and life means action. Keep your video moving, keep it dynamic. Otherwise, you might as well take black-and-white stills. When a director shouts "Action!" action is meant. Tape the processes of your library, the searching, the doing—the action.

Have your performers walk, reach for a book, put microfilm on a reader, type at a computer, climb stairs, open a map-case drawer. Varying your camera angles and scope is another method of instilling action.

Camera Angles

Move your movie by incorporating an aesthetic mixture of full shots, close-ups, medium shots, extreme close-ups. Show enough of a particular scene, but don't labor it. Usually about an eight-to-ten second hold on one scene is appropriate, not too short to eclipse information, not too long to bore. Use your camera zoom lens to advantage but not to annoyance. Zooming in and out about a half dozen times throughout a fifteen-minute video is plenty. More times than this shows an audience that you're enamored more with gadgetry than with the video.

Be aware that when you tilt a camera up and down you must do it slowly. The same is true when you pan from side to side. Keep both the tilts and pans to a minimum. Too many of either one turns an audience seasick in no time. One subtle trick: whenever possible, pan from left to right—the same direction the eye is trained to read in our culture.

Simplicity of Scenes

Keep your scenes simple and uncluttered. Backgrounds should be as plain as possible in order not to overwhelm the principal subject. Tell a story of your library as effectively and straightforwardly as you can manage. On tape the information on a catalog card or computer screen is not only displayed by the written words and symbols on this card but also by the technique with which you tape it. Simplify, simplify.

How you fill a picture frame is important. The composition of scenes in a video may be improved by a few simple shifts in camera angle. The following includes some fundamentals to remember when you're placing the camera:

- Library signs that are not three-dimensional should be taped straight on. A side angle will distort an image.

- Give your performers free space about their bodies in close-ups. Don't frame them with half their heads missing.

- Have all persons visible, especially their faces. Don't hide one behind another. Remember: people are interested in people.

- Balance your picture frame with angles that draw the eye into the picture. Avoid absolute symmetry. It's heavy, boring, and artificial.

- Always place someone or something familiar in the foreground when taping a large mass of a subject. This provides a sense of depth and a visual measuring stick in any large-scale scene.

As you work with a camera, you'll discover more shortcuts of your own. A feel of making a video provides you with the subtle insights of creativity, of manipulating camera, video-tape, lights, actors, sets, sunlight, chairs, newspapers, signs, passers-by and all the other parts that are shifted and molded into a comprehensive whole. If you're any kind of a maker at all, you'll find videotaping challenging and enjoyable.

Titles

Identification of your video is important. The creation of titles at the beginning of a tape is an almost separate art in itself. For beginners, however, the simplest is probably the easiest. Stick-on letters placed on a piece of colored paper may be done quickly. Just keep the titles short and unconfusing. You may require several sets of titles:

Title of the film	Narrated by [name]
Produced by [institution]	Year
Directed by [name]	"The End"

You may wish to add a bit of serendipity to the titles. They are, after all, the first images your audience sees. One interesting technique is to have the letters "spell themselves out" on the screen. To do this, draw a faint straight line on a piece of background paper. Pin the paper to a wall and secure the camera on a tripod in one immovable place. Press the camera shutter one-half second, or one frame if the camera is so equipped. Stick the first letter of the title on the paper. Press the shutter a half second. Add the next letter and expose the tape again. Continue to do the same until the entire line of words is completed. The end effect on the screen will be one letter after another rapidly appearing to spell out the titles.

Another trick is to take a sheet of thick clear plastic and paste the title on it. Then place these letters on the invisible plastic in front of an appropriate background. Move the camera in close to the titles, and shoot the scene while you read the words twice to yourself, the usual measuring standard. The end effect of this will be the letters of the titles being superimposed over whatever background you choose: the plastic sheet will not show.

Finishing Work

The mechanics of editing the visuals, adding voice-over narration, and overlaying music depend on the equipment you use, on whether or not you have visual and audio insert editing capability. New designs in the fast-growing video field make the finishing work continually easier. For example, Videonics offers editing units called DirectED and ProED that are compatible with nearly any camcorder and VCR. These computerized editing machines for videos also generate title graphics and special effects, all operated by wireless remote control.

Whatever equipment you use to make your final master videotape from which copies will be made, edit carefully and ruthlessly. Remove any glitches or shakes of the camera. Remove any scene, no matter how appealing, that does not move the video toward your goal. Fight the impulse to become enamored with a particular scene; if it doesn't fit the overall storytelling line of direction, obliterate it. Any tell-nothing scenes, such as a performer's walking endlessly up a section of stairs, can be shortened or eliminated. Video time may easily compress real time, which is a dramatic convention of the medium. Keep your scenes quick and interesting.

Once you think a final tape is finished, watch it again critically. A good video is a tight video, one that has no unnecessary slow and soft spots, one that has all unrelated scenes edited out, not in. Be aware of the flow of the storyline and the transitions from scene to scene, and alert for any long, boring sections. You've been through the creative process with the script and taping. Now don your critical cap to shape the video into something smooth, logical, and comprehensive.

Match the narration to the finished visuals, not the reverse. Your script was written weeks before the video was finished, and now some scenes may have changed somewhat, requiring a different narration. Expect this. A script, once again, is merely a guide. In a primarily visual medium, an image is more important than a voice. Therefore, voice must take second place in priority and be rearranged according to the final editing. This basic procedure saves innumerable headaches and unbelievable consternation over fitting tape to a written script. Remember: fit voice to image.

Background music adds a dimension to any video and is worth the trouble of careful selection and editing. Music should be selected with the understanding that it will be background music and nothing more. It must not overwhelm the narration or the visual images. The music should be subtle and complementary. Blatant rhythms or recognizable old warhorse symphonies will detract an audience from the real message of the video. Soft jazz is often acceptable.

Whatever the final changes are, keep in mind that all these details and decisions should be aimed toward the first goal of your video. Parts of your video should not stand out for their own sake but be integrated for the final effect—the library appearing as a welcoming place to help people with their minds and hearts.

FILM SLIDES

Far less expensive than videotapes in time, money, logistics, and energy are slides. A color-slide sequence may still be quite effective in generating interest in your library.

The Library Camera

Every library should stock its own 35mm camera, if not to produce slide/tape promotional programs then certainly to record a pictorial history of events and changes in a library. The 35mm camera may be used for promotional slides of your library on television. It may also be used to take black-and-white photographs that can be enlarged for newspaper publicity, brochures, and displays. Modern computerized cameras are extremely easy to use with their built-in light meters, simple focusing, automatic loading and rewinding of the film. Also, the high-speed, very light-sensitive transparency film virtually eliminates the need for flash lighting. But the important consideration in picture taking is the person behind the camera, not the intricate behind-the-lens metering. Imagination, not hundreds of dollars, produces the results. When good, 35mm color transparencies are used again and again, the cost per viewer becomes extremely low.

The Same Principles

The fundamental principles of making a tape also govern the making of a slide/tape presentation. Think carefully about what you want to accomplish. Preliminary planning is as important in structured picture taking as it is in putting a videotape together. Then write a script and follow it.

The key to good slides is simplicity. Keep the pictures extremely simple. You want your audience to absorb certain isolated bits of information from each slide when it appears on the screen. The accumulation of these bits of information is the message you wish to convey.

Vary the Scope

By deliberately planning your slide production beforehand, you eliminate a great deal of wasted time by moving directly to each segment of a script at the time you take the pictures. Remember that you are dealing with still photographs. Vary the scope of your shots so that an audience doesn't become numbed by seeing one long shot after another. For example, show: 1) a long shot of your library building; 2) a close shot of the name of your library; 3) a medium shot of patrons entering the building; 4) a medium shot of a librarian (smiling!) next to a welcome sign; 5) a close shot of "New Books" signs; 6) a close shot of covers of best-sellers; 7) a long shot of patrons at the librarian's desk.

Select for Excellence

Once you receive the transparencies from the processor, selection and sequencing the slides is relatively simple in comparison with editing videotape. Above all, maintain a sense of excellence when it comes time to put the slides in order. If a particular slide is out of focus, throw it in the wastebasket. If another one is awkwardly composed, throw it out—ruthlessly. Don't end up with a series of six perfect slides and ruin it with a bad seventh. Your audience will remember this seventh slide longer than the previous six. It will jar and disturb and negate the effectiveness of the others. Take the extra time to reshoot pictures or add others to the series if you think the production needs them.

Vary the Timing

Timing is important when you match a script with slides. You're dealing with still pictures, but you can create an illusion of movement by varying the time you hold each slide on the screen. Some long-shot slides may have very much visual information in them and will therefore require a longer hold on the screen for an audience to absorb all that is available. Don't cut such a slide short. Others, as close shots, may have only one word ("Welcome") and will not need the same time on the screen.

In other words, keep the slides moving according to the information content they hold. The eye absorbs much more than the ear in the same amount of time. Take advantage of this. Few slides in a fast-paced, interesting presentation should take ten seconds or more on the screen. Most will take about five or six seconds.

Dissolve   Overlapping the end of one scene with the beginning of the next

Emulsion   Light-sensitive chemical on the cellulose acetate film base; dull side of roll of film

F-stop   Numbers, such as *F-8,* that indicate the size of the opening of the aperture

Fade   Gradual rather than abrupt darkening toward complete black on the tape; can be used in either direction of black, as "Fade in" to scene or "Fade out" of scene

Focal Length   Distance from central point of the lens to the film

Foreground   Setting or subject nearest camera

Light Meter   Used to measure intensity of light on a scene in order to determine the F-stop and at what shutter speed to set the camera

Long Shot   Usually an all-encompassing scene

Medium Shot   A relatively mid-distance shot

Pan   A sweeping horizontal move of the camera to follow a moving subject or photograph a scene larger than the camera can hold in one position

Parallax   Difference between what is seen through the viewfinder of a camera and what is actually photographed, usually slight

Props   Movable equipment to add reality to a scene

Rough-cut   Videotape barely edited

Script

Written details of camera angles, action of subjects, narration, location, etc.

Shot

One exposure run of the camera

Storyboard

Visual outline of the story line of the videotape or slide production; narration is usually written near or on the same card as the hand-drawn pictures of proposed scenes

Sync

To match the sound with the action of the videotape

Tilt

A sweeping vertical move of the camera, such as focusing on the trunk of a tree and following the line of the tree to the top

Tripod

Three-legged mount for eliminating hand movement of camera when filming

Zoom

A rapid movement of the focal length of the lens in order to enlarge or shrink the scope of a scene, as in zooming from a long shot to a close shot without stopping the scene or the camera

11 Book Sales

Libraries are not book stores, but what reader passes up a book bargain? Not only do book sales produce money for special projects or direct additions to the general budget, they also instill public awareness that libraries can extend their purview and accommodation. Book sales at libraries are a natural adjunct of service for patrons. Library users, habitual or casual, are browsers strolling the aisles and glancing at titles in hopes of a good find. It's the same for book buyers, making book sales at libraries congenial and intriguing to the public.

Weed (But Sell Not Locally)

Every library now and then needs to thin its collection of books and other material to make room for new titles, eliminate dead wood, or redirect its collection. The criteria for weeding are left to individual librarians, but a general principle that helps avoid public relations trouble is—Don't sell the discards locally.

If you do place your discards in a library book sale, chances are good that someone who frequents your library will see the discards and ask, "How can the library sell its collection like that? Is this why I can never find the books I used to check out? Tax money is spent to buy books for everybody's use, not to turn around and sell them for nobody's use? I was shocked to see a book stamped with the name of our own library being sold right here for profit. How many other good books have been sold? Which ones were they? Are they being replaced? Which ones are taking their place? Since our taxes are buying the books for the library, why are we paying for them again? Who decides what books from our library are to be sold? How do they decide?" On and on.

You can always counter the prickly question with answers

that justify the sale of discards by referring to job descriptions of librarians hired for educated decision-making and to sustain the cerebral health of the library. It will do little good, especially set against a particular book brought up by a very particular patron.

Better to weed the collection with judicious eye and quiet lips, and then place the discards beyond the madding local crowd. For admirable librarians who die a little when any book whatsoever is burned or shredded, donate discards to hospitals, nursing homes, and other libraries, or sell them to used book dealers on the far horizon.

Sell Donations

People donate books to their local library for many reasons. Perhaps they too cannot bear to cast a book into the trash heap or incinerate it with impunity. They may have a special affinity with the library and wish to contribute in a small way to its continuing vitality, or they simply don't know what to do with books they wish to remove from their homes.

Also, many times relatives clean out a home of a family member who has died and they don't know how to assess the value of books. They may think of the local librarian as someone with expertise in evaluating and appreciating books. They may offer to donate the collection in toto, as a way of getting rid of books without destroying them.

Whatever the reason, this provides a fine opportunity for librarians. By all means, go to the home and take a look. The collection may be pedestrian or priceless. Either way, you embody the extension of the local library beyond its walls, and in turn may indeed discover a means of improving your services within the walls.

Be sure, however, to make clear to those donating that you as the librarian must have the ultimate decision as to how these books are to be used. Some titles may be included in the library collection; certain titles, after all, may fill gaps or replace tattered editions. But also make plain that some of these donated books will in all likelihood be sold at the next book sale sponsored by the library. Emphasize, however, that the money made from these donated books will go to the benefit of the library. This assures those offering you their private collection that their gift will—for certain—benefit the public. Few transactions generate more ire and disappointment than the donation of a once-prideful collection to a public institution, only to discover later that the gifts were sold away to a mingling mob. Make it doubly clear what you intend to do with the collection before you accept and sell the books, not after. A receipt on library stationery stating that you have discretion in the disposal of the books insures this understanding.

Examine Discards and Donations

Fear of discarding valuable books plagues conscientious librarians, but judgments have to be made in the context of the overall library program, collection, and time available. The very least you can do for the protection of your library resources is to examine, if only briefly, your discards and donations. You might open a treasure chest.

Ann Geisel, director of the Peterborough (N.H.) Town Library, the first tax-supported free library in the world, tells this tale of several years ago. She was weeding the art and music section and came upon a book that no one had checked out for many years. The book was in Italian and printed in Italy. When she opened the cover, she saw a photograph of the composer with the handwritten words, "With the composer's compliments, December 10, 1910. New York." It was signed: "Giacomo Puccini." Said Geisel, "Bingo!"

She wrote an explanatory letter to several rare book and antique dealers, stating that she would sell the book to the highest bidder and giving them a month to reply. One dealer offered her $300, and she added the money to the special projects fund of the library.

Sorting and Pricing

When donated books arrive and upon examination are found not needed for the general library collection, they are best sorted according to subject. This can be done either on workroom shelves or in cartons. Those that are appropriate for a book sale are separated from others destined elsewhere. This process is usually year long, since book sales normally are scheduled for one or two days once a year.

This is also the time to separate donations according to appropriate pricing. Often private collections contain expensive art books, which would be shuddering to sell for a dollar at a library book fest. These obviously more expensive titles should be placed alongside library discards and listed for book dealer bidding and other destinations.

One effective way to distribute the more expensive donated books and discards is to list them by subject area. Then send copies of these lists to a number of used- and rare-book dealers who might be interested in such titles. Offer the titles on a highest-bidder basis. Most likely, you will receive many offers covering parts of the list and end up packing and shipping a dozen books here, two dozen there. But you'll get rid of the lot and make some money at the same time.

Pricing titles for the book sale should be based on moving the most books possible. That means accepting a very low price, which could start at seventy-five cents for hardcovers, a quarter for paperbacks. The object is to generate a sense of service to the reading community, not merely profit for the library; an excitement for book lovers, not turning the library into a book store.

Library book sales must first of all be a generous offering to the public. Let the moneymaking for the library be well understood to be secondary. You might, as some librarians do, reduce the prices as the day progresses and the choice samplings diminish. The Hancock (N.H.) Public Library, for example, ends its book sale by offering a bagful of books for fifty cents. Not only does this keep the sale going but it clears out as many books as possible. This way librarians avoid dealing with the remainders.

Advertise

You have no book sale if you have no book buyers, who will show up only if they know about the event. So get the word out as much as you can.

The easiest and first outlet is your library column in the local newspaper, if you've established one over the years. Two or three months ahead of the sale you might include a few invitations for residents to donate books for the sale. This is also the time to inform the public that donations, not books from the library collection, are for sale. Then, a month ahead of the sale, repeated mentions of the big date in successive columns reinforce the event in the reader's mind. One way of doing this is to print a two-liner in bold-face type at the bottom of the column, listing the date, time, and place.

Do indeed consider the sale an annual event, not a passing incident. By all means, deliver press releases to local newspapers and radio stations in and around the community. Be sure to promote the sale beyond your immediate area. Book lovers will drive miles to neighboring towns or cities for a good sale, a reason that wide promotional coverage is important. Look to more people than just your own library patrons.

Design large, clear, professional-looking posters with all the pertinent information—name of your library, the words "Book Sale," date, time, place, and a hint of a big selection at small prices. Distribute and display the posters as widely as feasible in shop windows, marketplace bulletin boards, community centers. A good way to ease the distribution time and trouble is to have a bookmobile or state delivery van leave the posters at branch libraries and nearby town libraries for posting.

On the day of the sale, attract those passersby who, astoundingly, failed to learn about the sale beforehand. Simply place posters, signs, and colorful balloons at strategic points outside the library—on telephone poles, walls, tree trunks. Then, after the sale, make use of the opportunity for a follow-up public relations release. Turn your sales figures into a news story. Of course, you must keep records for this at the time of the sale, but it is of interest to the public how much money was made for the library, how many books were sold, how many people attended, how the sale compared with the one last year. Keep in mind that a book sale, beyond its ostensible purpose, is a chance to raise the good name, image, and idea of your library in the public consciousness.

The Big Event

Rare- and used-book dealers will learn of your sale soon and probably ask to be included on your future mailing list. If you don't have a list of people to be notified of the sale, start one. Book dealers can be a source of a hefty portion of your sales. In fact, book dealers will line up at your starting time, and when the doors open, stampede to the books. This is great for the sale and immediately injects excitement for everyone involved.

Throughout the sale, a primary purpose is to reestablish your library as a comfortable, enjoyable place to look at books, buy a few, and go home remembering the library as a place to return for another easy visit. Be free and easy with price reductions and giveaways. Cut-throat capitalism is not the guiding principle here. You'll make some money for the library, but more important you'll make good feelings and friends.

12 Book Talks and Readings

A goal of public relations is to generate interest in the content of your library and entice the public into the building. Once the people are inside, you can rely on other means to create the feeling in them that your place is pleasant and easy-going, a center of activity where they can find informative, entertaining material to enjoy there or check out to take home. Book talks and library-sponsored readings by poets and writers are good outreach programs for this enticement. They require time and effort, but the benefits are solid and long-lasting.

BOOK TALKS

Impelled by the central philosophy of your profession, to be of service to those who request it, means giving book talks to anyone who wants them. More than likely, the requests will come from other than the usual individual library users. They'll include an interesting array of groups—American Association of Retired People, school children, parent-teacher associations, church groups, women's clubs, fraternal organizations. These offer an important outlet for presenting the library and its resources to highly focused groups that in turn can cement support for your library in the future. The return goes far beyond your direct involvement with them. If at all possible, say yes to each and every request.

Gearing to the Audience

Assessing your audience makes book talks easier and more fun for both you and the listeners. An optimum length of time is one hour for most groups; this is usually the time allotted by groups that schedule regular programs of outside speakers. But perhaps a thirty-minute program would be better for a group at a nursing home or young children in a classroom. It depends on how you judge the age, education, and book interest of the group.

If you're part of a regular round-robin program and talk about books to the same group every month, then the shorter side of an hour would be more rewarding. On the other hand, if you get a chance to be on a Kiwanis program once a year, then you might let the program go the full hour, with maybe a question period spilling over if interest remains high.

Matching Books with the Group

Part of the art of giving book talks is to select titles that have the most appeal to the largest number of members of a particular group. Books about high finance on Wall Street are not a sterling choice for third graders. A title on grandparenting, however, would probably fit a nursing home audience. An AARP audience is not likely to favor books with sex, violence, or alley language, while a fraternal organization would probably perk up at hearing about books on business successes and projections of economic trends.

A mixed list of titles is always good if it seems to fit the group. Most listeners are fascinated by biographies and how other people live their lives. Biographies are always sure-fire interest igniters. You may be asked beforehand to review a certain title which is close to the heart of the president of the group; do so by all means. And sometimes it may be particularly appropriate to talk about old favorites and classics that for some reason may be currently in the news.

How to Do It

Good book talks require good preparation. This means you'll read about twenty or thirty new titles so that you'll know what you're talking about. A mistake that isn't always obvious is to stand up before your audience and repeat a review of the book that some critic wrote. Not only will you personally be uninformed about the book, but the review may be less than trustful and competent, distorting the subject or tone of the book. Read the books yourself and make your own judgments.

Bring the books to the meeting. Hold them up for all to see as you talk about them. Depending on the title, you may want to read parts of a book to underscore your comments. Read some of the beautiful language, what is funny, something enchanting or touching. But keep the excerpts you read aloud short and sweet. And move on to the next title.

Some titles contain material that you can summarize and have your audience on the edge of their seats. For instance, giving the background of the book and author of *Small Town Living* adds to the drama of what you're about to present. This particular book tells the story of a salesman who fell asleep by the side of a road, woke up, and saw two men carrying a dead calf and throwing it into the river. The next day he saw in the local paper that the town bully had been murdered and thrown in the river. The salesman realized then what he had actually seen. He didn't do anything about it but carried the story around with him for years, until finally, before he died, he revealed the murder to his son. His son, an English teacher, later wrote his father's story. This is the kind of book talk that gets people in the audience scribbling notes so they can go to the library and read it for themselves—the best kind of reward you can ask for.

After you've finished presenting the titles, open the rest of the time for questions, which may center on the books or stray to other aspects of your library. It makes no difference; you *are* the library during this program and what you say and how you present yourself is the real heart of the program.

At the tail end of your allotted time, hand out a list of the titles, authors, and call numbers of the books you discussed. (Of course, you have prepared this list in advance.) Print it attractively on library stationery that includes your open hours and the name of someone to answer questions when the individual members of the audience arrive in search of these—and other—books.

Why Do It

Giving book talks generates peripheral rewards beyond the immediate pleasure of seeing people respond to what you're offering them. First of all, it promotes reading at a time when the general public is becoming more aware of the degeneration of literacy in this country. Book talks help combat illiteracy and its dangers (not being able to read labels on medicine bottles or household poisons), risks (inability to read contracts), inconveniences (undecipherable menus), perspectives (not being able to read and verify history), and pleasures (limiting the expansion and exploration of private new worlds and imagination).

In addition, book talks keep the idea, concept, and alternative of reading in the forefront, reminding people that books offer extraordinary opportunities that they may have forgotten because of the swampy habit of TV staring.

Book talks are especially effective at emphasizing new titles and are a way to develop reading lists right away. Often after a book talk a library new-book shelf is inundated with people who are signing up to reserve titles they have heard about. This justifies the purchase of these titles better than any other way.

Also, if you present book talks to groups that might not ordinarily be exposed to books and libraries, to people who might not use the library at all, you can use the time to explain what else the library offers—records, tapes, large-print books, maps, magazines, reference materials of all kinds, video cassettes, and the rest.

Book talks get you out of the building to meet people you wouldn't normally meet, which has its good and bad points. You'll discover how much the general public is ill-educated about libraries—far more than you may anticipate. This can be frightening and lead you to ponder whether you're doing the job you thought you were. You may think that the general public is fully aware that their library offers them magazines to check out and read at home. Many people don't know this, or know about many other services you thought were obvious to them. Book talks give you the chance to explain these services and resources, not just to non-users but to library users as well. Many people are programmed to know where something is and they go right for it, not realizing that the library provides many other options.

Ann Geisel, director of the Peterborough (N.H.) Town Library, is a firm believer in book talks and an expert book talker. She recognizes the extra rewards of instilling interest in books. "I don't care what brings them in the library," she says. "It doesn't have to be just for a book. If they're interested in a book on tape or a video, even if they're using the hall downstairs, just as long as they're in here using the facility to see what we look like and to feel comfortable, and to feel ownership. Then when at town meeting they're about to vote on my budget, even if they're not readers, they'll say, Oh, yeah, library, nice place. You really do have to promote the library, and you can't do it enough."

SPONSORING READINGS

As an educational institution, your library is a natural place to hold lectures, discussion groups, and readings. Most likely, your state has a council or agency of the humanities that offers matching grants for round table series or symposia headed by a university professor. Perhaps your state library co-sponsors programs designed for individual libraries around the state. Or maybe you wish to sponsor a reading and discussion program developed by the Great Books Foundation in Chicago.

The content and focus of these programs may differ, but many of the principles and methods of getting the public interested in the events, and keeping the participants enthusiastic, are similar.

Here's how the Peterborough (N.H.) Town Library sponsored a successful reading by local poets and writers.

Organizing the Program

Connecting people with ideas requires imaginative planning. Ann Geisel, director of the Peterborough Library, and

Julia Older, a poet and writer in the area, pooled their interests and came up with a format that seemed likely to appeal to a large number of people. As library director, Geisel would apply for a National Endowment for the Arts grant, while Older would put together a team of poets and writers.

They decided to hold a three-part series of readings in a relatively open area of the periodical section, instead of downstairs in the stark function room. They thought that the books-and-magazines setting in the main part of the library would provide a better atmosphere for the program. Older assembled a list of poets and writers living in the state. Then Geisel sent them letters asking whether they would be interested in participating and what their fees would be. Some gave readings for high fees and eliminated themselves, but most accepted, because the list was put together by someone familiar with the poets and writers. Knowing exactly who would be on the program was necessary before applying for the NEA grant.

To structure the series and the three individual reading nights to attract the broadest audience, Geisel and Older paired the six participants this way: two poets (Jane Kenyon and Charles Simic), two fiction writers (Edith Milton and Ernest Hebert), two poets (Julia Older and Sydney Lea). Each reading, with female and male authors, was scheduled one week apart at 7:30 p.m.

Getting a Grant

With the program planned and the participants committed, Geisel filled out the forms for NEA matching funds under its Audience Development Grant program. "By offering a series of readings by contemporary writers of both poetry and fiction," she wrote in the application, "the library hopes to expand the public's awareness of the talents in this area, and its appreciation of these art forms." She pointed out that, although Peterborough had a population of 5,000, the library served many neighboring towns, increasing its service area to 20,000 people.

The total matching grant was for $3,000. Geisel made sure

that the expenses for publicity, printing, and refreshment (PR for the important gastrointestinal track) was a third of the NEA grant. She also made part of the grant an in-kind contribution of the library for purchasing titles of the poets and writers that were not yet part of the library collection.

After the traditional bureaucratic wait, the grant was awarded. What until then was a hopeful possibility became an emerging reality.

Keeping the Participants Informed

Good public relations includes not only the public at large but also those involved in your programs. Keeping participants informed of the progress of the programs keeps them confident in your handling of the readings and enthusiastic as a participant. When Geisel received word that the NEA had funded the reading series, she immediately sent a short handwritten note to each of the six poets and writers, telling them of the official acceptance of the proposal. She suggested that each of the readers bring copies of their books to sell; someone from the library staff would handle the sales of the books after each reading. She also included the NEA letter of agreement between the poet or writer and the NEA stipulating the time and place of the reading, plus that they should write a brief evaluation of the program and send it to the program director.

All-Important Publicity

Next, Geisel and Older assembled a comprehensive list of newspapers, radio stations, and outlets for posters. They decided to give the series the title "Authorized Hour," which would appear in all news releases and posters.

Their list of newspapers and radio stations included the deadlines of each paper and the name of the editor or feature writer likely to deal with such events. Newspapers close by were listed separately so that the releases could be delivered in person. The papers farther away were listed for releases to be sent by mail.

They realized that half of the participants lived well beyond the circulation of the four local newspapers. So they included news releases and photos to their home town papers. This gave the poets and writers publicity as well as the library.

News releases were also sent to the major statewide newspaper, the state Commissioner on the Arts, English departments of colleges and universities, area-wide public libraries, bookstores, and the State Library Newsletter.

Careful planning was thought out ahead of deadlines. Instead of one wrap-up, all-inclusive news release for the three-part series, one release and photos for each program were sent to the papers and (no photos) radio stations. These were printed or announced immediately prior to each scheduled weekly reading. In this way, each reading received a more concentrated focus and gave the library three times as much publicity as only one general release would give. Also, more room in each news release was available to present the backgrounds of the two participants for that week.

Posters were displayed prominently in the Peterborough Library a month ahead of the series. In addition, posters were delivered to nearby college and public libraries, supermarkets, bookstores, stationery stores, nursing homes, hospitals, and any other store or agency that would display them. They were printed on stiff board and titled, like all the other publicity releases, "Authorized Hour," next to a stylized drawing of a chair and window in a "Poet's loft." The information was brief and to the point, clearly printed, and with large type emphasized the names of the participants. It read, "N.H. Poets and Fiction Writers. The Peterborough Town Library presents a Series of Readings." The dates, times, and names of the readers of each weekly reading were listed. The bottom lines read, "Series Free and Open to the Public at the Peterborough Town Library. Funded by the National Endowment for the Arts."

Preparing for a Reading

A few days before the scheduled readings, telephone each participant to confirm the date and time, which is an excuse on your part to reconfirm the commitment on their part. Now is the time to ask the readers if they prefer to stand behind a lectern or in front of it, to sit on a stool or a chair.

On the day of the reading, have ready whatever it takes to please the participants before they arrive. Start early. Avoid last-minute rushes and crises. Do your rushing ahead of the reading so that you'll be calm and settled when the audience and participants arrive. This means that you should have the table displaying the books of the poets and writers ready many hours ahead of schedule, their stool or lectern in place, the chairs for the audience lined up, the lighting long ago decided and—most important—tested (and a microphone tested too, if one is used).

Usually, the audience lingers after a reading to talk with friends or with the participants. Instead of bringing refreshments from the backroom or kitchen, have them ready and waiting behind the audience or to the side. This eliminates any possibility of spilling the goods as you come out. (Refreshments at one reading in Peterborough included a platter of home-baked madeleines.) By having everything ready and in place, including refreshments, the audience and participants will recognize that you're well prepared, that all is nice and secure, everyone relaxed and confident.

All these details were taken care of for the "Authorized Hour" at the Peterborough Library readings. Preparations were done well ahead of schedule so that the evening opened with style and ended with success.

Follow-Up

After the readings, thanking each participant with a short note is a basic courtesy that lets the poets and writers know that their effort, time, and travel are appreciated. It's also a good time to briefly describe the positive reactions of the audience and to relay any comments that came your way and that may not have reached the poets and writers.

After the Peterborough reading, Geisel pointed out that following the "Authorized Hour" the audience was highly charged. People milled around and talked to the poets and writers longer than at most other library events. The effects of a well-planned and executed barrage of publicity were evident. Members of the audience came from twelve different surrounding towns, not merely from Peterborough where the event was held. Some from Peterborough, in fact, were not familiar library users.

Reactions of the poets and writers themselves are indicative of how well you planned and served the events. For this particular reading, Geisel received comments from the participants that included, "I have read all over the country at universities and colleges, and I must say that the communal feeling of the Peterborough reading was especially refreshing." "It was wonderful to look over the rows of faces, and to see people sitting on the floor, lurking among the stacks, spilling down the staircase, in that happy collegiate abandon which usually means that they're having a good time when they only expected to have a virtuous one." "Every chair in the library was used, including pint-sized children's chairs. A media blitz does work. All-out publicity is terribly important."

13   Simple but Important

No matter how simple an idea may appear, if it is used effectively at the right time and in the right place, the idea when joined with other small ones can have a valuable cumulative benefit for your library.

You don't need stupendous fiery rockets to attract notice, but you do need to get ideas out of your head and into your heart and hand.

Put Them to Work

Little things mean a lot in this world of corporate hugeness. The personal touches, the unusual slants, the unexpected enthusiasms, the simple gimmicks and games, lend themselves to creating an atmosphere of caring about the people you serve and making it easier and more pleasant for the people to be served.

The first step in the right direction is to use the word *please*. Train your clerks to use the word and mean it at all times in dealing with patrons. Unfortunately, in some cases you'll have to train your professionals to use it, too. Most of all, redesign your signs to include the word. Please remember, your library is not a military installation.

Which of the two below shows respect for people:

DO NOT SMOKE	PLEASE DO NOT SMOKE

The answer should be obvious. One important word— *Please*—in your appropriate signs can make a subtle but telling difference in how well your library is received and enjoyed.

Fact Sheet

Every library should have a basic fact sheet of its facilities and resources. This sheet should be readily available to hand to patrons who ask statistical questions about the library, or inserted in new-patron packets, or given to newspaper editors with each news release, or mailed to new residents, or used in many other ways to supply fundamental information about your library.

A fact sheet is best presented in outline form, uncluttered and easy to read. The content should not include a detailed history of a library nor elaborate plans for future expansion and buildings. Keep a fact sheet as simple as possible. Make it serve its purpose, so that it will be used rather than discarded.

A fact sheet will be a reminder to patrons of what your library is like once they're beyond your walls. Your library should be considered professional, shipshape, and sophisticated. A one-page print job by photo offset or desktop computer publishing is less expensive than you may realize and will give you a far better product to represent your library than photocopying a typewritten sheet.

Here's a sample fact sheet:

Garfield Public Library
2126 Atlantic Blvd.
Northridge, Idaho
Phone: 743-4411 (circulation desk)
743-4412 (reference desk)

Hours: 9–9 Monday through Saturday
           12–9 Sunday

Circulation: Books, 3 weeks
               Magazines, 1 week
               Phonograph records, 3 weeks
               Films, 2 days

Volumes: 75,000 adult books
           10,000 juvenile
           210 adult magazine titles
           35 juvenile magazine titles

Phonograph records: 500

Films: 350 (16mm)

Building: Constructed in 1949
6,000 square feet
Seating for 80 individuals

Staff: 4 professional librarians
8 clerks
6 student helpers

The Light Touch

A light touch now and then does wonders for the spirit of your patrons, staff, and yourself. Take a few chances with small signs about the library. Have one of your more artistic staff members hand-letter small cards that can be taped to the wall at strategic points. Here are a few possibilities that could show patrons their librarians are enjoying themselves and like their work:

Over the pencil sharpener:
"COURTESY OF WILLIAM SHAKESPEARE, JOHN STEINBECK, ISAAC ASIMOV, AND ALL AUTHORS WHO MAKE THIS LIBRARY POSSIBLE."

Beside the water fountain:
"PROS AND CONS OF FLUORIDATION OF WATER AVAILABLE AT CALL NUMBER 614.5."

Beside the newspapers:
"WILL ROGERS SAID ALL HE EVER KNEW WAS WHAT HE SAW IN THE PAPERS. WE SUBSCRIBE TO TWENTY-SIX OF THEM."

Over the photocopying machine:
"THIS MACHINE IS FOR YOUR CONVENIENCE AND OUR HEADACHE."

On the catalog cabinet:
"THE CATALOG OF WHAT'S INSIDE THIS BUILDING IS
THE LARGEST KEY IN THE WORLD."

You don't have to stop here with such signs. Use one of
your large front windows. Now who wouldn't stop a moment
to consider a big bold red-letter sign in a self-respecting
library that in one giant four-letter word read:

$$\boxed{\text{SALE}}$$

If you feel nervous about this alone, you could print in
small letters:

75,000 BOOKS IMMEDIATELY AVAILABLE ON FREE
SHORT- AND LONG-TERM LOAN. COLLATERAL: LI-
BRARY CARD.

Small Conveniences

Make the use of your library as convenient to patrons as
possible. After all, you want them to enjoy their visits and
find them so profitable and time-saving that they will not only
return but will recommend the library to their friends.

Some of these conveniences to the patron might turn out to
be irritating inconveniences to the library clerks and professionals, but then, the users, not librarians, are number one.

Pencil and Paper

Nothing is more frustrating than for a person to come to a
library and suddenly find he or she has no paper on which to
copy notes. Prepare for this inevitable catastrophe. Make sure
that your circulation desk has a couple reams of cheap but
standard size 8½" × 11" paper, one ream ruled, one ream
plain.

Forget the leftover scratch paper. Use this yourself, if you must. If patrons ask, give the people a decent piece of paper. This may cost the library a few dollars a month, if that much. On the other hand, it will save individuals from moving about the library and disturbing others in their quest for, please, something to write on.

Besides this, stock a box of pencils behind the front desk. Have the pencils ready on request and distribute them pleasantly. People forget pencils and pens or don't anticipate that they will need them at a library when they first leave home. Anticipate their needs instead of frustrating them further.

More people will return the pencils than not. Even if you do lose some, count the loss as public relations expenditures. Whatever you do, keep in mind that some people really and truly are motivated by such thoughts as not bothering with a library because they never have pencils. Little things mean a lot.

Rainbags

On rainy days your library will win friends, too, if it provides plastic rainbags as standard fare for patrons to carry their books home or to the car. Besides being a welcome convenience to a reader, plastic sacks protect books from water damage. Sturdy bags may be ordered cheaply enough by the multigross from suppliers. Don't miss an opportunity for public relations either. Be sure to have printed on the outside of the bags something along the line of: "For your convenience. Garfield Public Library." Maybe a local bank will sponsor the bags and save you further expense.

Convenient Hours

Convenience for a patron should also prompt you to staff your library at hours in line with the needs of most users. This means that public libraries that may only afford to stay open eight or nine hours each day might switch the time from 9–5 to 12–9 in the evening. This covers the time period most likely to attract the most people throughout the day. Many libraries around the country find this more beneficial to the people of their communities. More libraries, too, are opening the doors on Sundays, normally a workless day of relaxation that may easily be used by the entire family for going to a library.

Public Telephones

Convenience for a patron means providing a public telephone within easy access. Libraries are in the business of communication. They should provide whatever medium it takes to make library systems handy and modern. A small sign beside the telephone: FOR YOUR CONVENIENCE, saves a lot of questions at the front desk and at the same time notches some points in the public eye. Installing pay phones eliminates congestion at the library phones.

Drive-Up Windows

Some libraries are experimenting with drive-up windows similar to those that commercial banks have found popular. Typical Americans are in a hurry and use wheels as their solution. They eat in drive-in restaurants, pick up hamburgers and french fries at drive-through short-order stands, cash checks at drive-up bank windows, buy milk and bread at drive-in markets, grab a dozen doughnuts at a drive-in shop, and now pick up airplane tickets at drive-in travel agents. Why shouldn't typical Americans in a hurry drive-up to get books?

In lieu of remodeling your building, you could spread the word that patrons may order specific titles over the telephone and that by the time they arrive at the library the titles will be at the circulation desk stamped, dated, and ready to travel.

Book Lists

Perhaps a user has no idea what book to read. The old standby of book lists shouldn't be shunned. They come in handy for both the infrequent and the regular reader. Standard book lists that cover such fields as paperbacks in the home, or outstanding biographies, fiction, books on theater, and the like are what librarians know about and should produce for their patrons.

These can be effective, especially if your own lists are appropriate to the times and place. The lists can be as short as six or seven titles. All lists should be annotated briefly in some way.

Here are subject possibilities for lists:

- Works of authors who live in town or nearby

- Books that cover city and state histories

- State holidays that are explained and historically traced

- Books made into movies shown recently in local theaters

- Related readings on subject of historical movies shown locally

- Titles that enlighten a community controversy, such as rezoning, team teaching, pollution

- Home-improvement readings at springtime

- Travel books during the summer months

- Sports books during the Christmas season and New Year's Day

- Books on drugs when an issue arises in the community

- Titles around a theme of a well-publicized speech in town

- Further readings on a well-known playwright whose production was staged recently

Print these lists on long narrow strips of paper or on wide short pieces. Try to avoid a full $8\frac{1}{2}'' \times 11''$ size. The lists get more mileage if you do.

Try to get your book lists distributed inside and outside your library. Try anywhere people gather—grocery, hardware, and department stores, restaurants, banks. One way to help persuade managers of these places is to present them with appropriate lists. To the manager of a grocery store give lists on cookbooks; to a banker, lists on finance; a hardware-store owner, home improvement; a department-store manager, fashion; a restaurateur, wines. Appeal to their special interests.

Beyond the Walls

These are ways of reaching people who might not normally be as hypnotized as you are by the glory and grandeur of the library world. Many other ways are open as well. Advertising on buses or subways may cost money, but the unusualness of a commercial or public service message for libraries on a bus may hit passengers with a wallop.

Bumper stickers and lapel buttons are another comparatively inexpensive means of putting the library world or your particular library in the public mind. Distribute them at a circulation desk or mail at random to members of a community. Either way they extend your world beyond the front doors.

You can make your own graffiti or borrow some of these:

Casanova Was a Librarian

Read Books, Not This

Melville Dewey Was a Bookie

The Public Library Has a Four-Letter Word—Book

Bibliomaniacs Are Loose at the Public Library

Date the Public Library Tonight

612.6 Is a Three-Letter Word at the Library

The possibilities are endless, and poking fun at yourself and your field is healthy.

Door-to-Door

Another way of moving outside the public library walls to bring attention to what you have inside is to conduct a door-to-door campaign. Politicians perform this sometimes exhilarating self-promotion, usually to solid advantage. In the long run nothing succeeds like one-to-one personal contact.

Librarians may find it difficult to justify the time involved in such a project. Many library-aware student workers and clerks, however, would find such a project fun, interesting, and worthy of their youthful energy.

The ostensible purpose would be to canvass neighborhoods in search of members of households who do not have library cards. The students would be authorized to issue cards on the doorstep if desired. If the household already had library cards, then the students could distribute a single sheet listing new acquisitions of everything from mysteries to political science, videos to phonograph records. This way occupants have something concrete in hand to remind them of the library once the students leave the front porch. Such a campaign is far more effective than a mailing list (though a mailing list is much better than nothing at all).

Other Doors to the Public

Student workers could also peddle library cards, book lists, or promotional flyers at bus stops, airports, court houses, movie theaters, art exhibits, museums, supermarkets, department stores, civic centers, parks. Anywhere people gather in large numbers is fair territory for politely but effectively promoting your wares. Supply tourist bureaus with information about your library. The Chamber of Commerce should have on hand plenty of facts and figures about library facilities in the area to supply to prospective businesspeople and industrial management.

Countless institutions and agencies promote their products and services openly to the public. The Cancer Society does it. The President of the United States does it with White House television broadcasts. Why shouldn't librarians do it? Such campaigns may decrease the importance of the classic myths about libraries, but they certainly won't decrease interest in library resources.

Also, contact new residents in a community as soon as possible to see that they are supplied with a library card and information about procedures and resources. A list of new residents is usually obtained from City Hall.

"Welcome Wagons"

Many communities have organized welcoming committees or "Welcome Wagons" that greet new residents. Usually the operators of these welcoming committees have Chamber of Commerce information about a town and a set of coupons for discount prices at a number of businesses within the city limits. These are presented gratis and with goodwill to new residents. Your library cannot afford to miss being part of this welcoming-committee packet. If your town does have such a committee, be certain to track down the individuals who organize and run it. Provide them with library information and authorization to issue cards on their first visit to your new neighbors. A series of discount coupons means a new resident still must pay something. A library card is free—your first step in the right direction with newcomers.

Small Adventures

One library risked $20 to attract public attention, but it would have cost very many times this amount for a professional public relations consultant. Four five-dollar bills were placed in books at random in the library. Through radio and newspapers the public was told that the five-dollar bills were theirs if they happened to come across them while thumbing through a book. As a result, the library was unusually but not unexpectedly crowded with people thumbing through books—and checking them out. The library "lost" two of the five dollar bills but came out far ahead in public awareness of what the library had to offer its community.

Another library taped a five-second message that prefaced a recording of the time of day from the telephone company.

Every time anyone dialed the time on the phone came: "The North Star Borough Library is on the move. Visit it soon."

Classifieds

Libraries with small budgets but with lots of initiative may take out three- or four-line ads in the classified section of local newspapers. The ads are normally quite inexpensive in regular newspapers; in the throwaway shoppers they are nearly free. Placement in such an unlikely spot to promote libraries might return steady dividends far beyond hopes.

The ads could be very simple, such as:

Information on the drug issue at the Garfield Public Library.

Know what you're talking about. Garfield Public Library.

Best-sellers on free loan at the Public Library.

Lots of other information at the free public library.

Newsletters

One continuing outlet for library promotion is a newsletter, but be easy on yourself. Make it simple and make it monthly. A one-page newsletter printed on both sides with plenty of aesthetic white space should be sufficient for a starter.

Give your newsletter a refreshing name. Avoid the standard "Newsletter" or even "Garfield Public Library News." Instead, try something that stands on its own and is not necessarily tied directly to libraries. Some of these may be possibilities for you: *Tidings; 050; The Shelf; User-Peruser; Bibliomania.*

Identify your library in small print immediately beneath the title. The contents may include whatever you wish—new policies, personnel, acquisitions, and hopes; anecdotes; statistics; unusual gifts, best-sellers; humor; books that relate to current community events; perhaps a "letters to the editor" column.

Keep the style informal. Make it easy to ready quickly. your goal isn't to provide a piece of literature. Expect that 99 percent of your readers will discard the newsletter soon after they read it. This doesn't matter. Your goal is to make readers aware that the library exists, that progress is a keystone of your operations, that many activities are happening all the time. Your library is a place on the move, definitely a place to visit.

Try to have your newsletter printed professionally. The extra expense is worth the extra consideration your readers will give your product. Choose a distinctive color and stick to it. Regularity reinforces expectation in readers and identifies the product uniquely.

Limit the content. Restrain yourself. You will probably want to include more than is needed or will be read. Too much copy without enough white space produces a backlash effect in readers: they'll probably throw the publication away too soon. In the case of newsletters, too little said is often better than too much.

If you are not an accomplished artist, forget drawings. Amateurish drawings only detract from the overall effect. Keep it simple, keep it direct, and keep it honest.

Your newsletter can be sent to department offices, agencies of your community, businesses, schools, and homes. Your one-pager will not be the be-all and end-all of library promotion. On the other hand, it will be one more of the many simple outlets that, when added together, bring more notice, understanding, appreciation, and use of your library.

14   Support Your Local VIP's

Those who must rely on the public for one reason or another know the value of public opinion. You can't see public opinion, just as you can't see the atmosphere, but it's there. It pressures directions, changes attitudes, reverses dogmas. Public opinion had better be controlled as much as possible or, like a sudden shift in the wind, it may bowl over an institution or prominent person. Public opinion is this powerful. Automobile designers, politicians, proponents of fluoride-in-the-water, and other captives of the public posture understand its influence.

Word of Mouth

Advertising notwithstanding, the most potent factor in spreading public opinion is word of mouth. Experts in mass communications agree that what one person says to another on a one-to-one basis has more impact on the latter's opinions than what is read in magazines or heard on radio or television. Word of mouth. Person to person. Friend to friend. You know yourself how much more secure you feel when a novel is suggested to you by a colleague rather than a journal review, even if the suggestion is identical.

Publishers themselves reluctantly admit that the best advertising of any book is word of mouth. What people have to say about a recent title is extremely important to its long-run success. The same happens with library service. The opinion people have of your library, and what it does or does not do, plays a substantial role in how much the library is used and how effective a role it plays in the community. Public opinion may be wrong, but generally, when a certain opinion is widespread it is usually accurate. The real business of a library is to provide solid, progressive, user-oriented service, not public opinion. Yet it is incumbent on you as a professional librarian proud of your field to reinforce the popular view people have of your library, whether the people are of a community at large, students and teachers on campus and playground, or specialized personnel in a company building.

Opinion Makers

Public opinion is potent. It usually works from the top down. Every community, campus, or company has some people who influence what others think and feel. These are the opinion makers, the people of quality, force, power, insight, expertise, intelligence, friendliness, experience, of any other quality that sets them beyond the mainstream and gives them an aura of authority.

Get to know opinion makers. They are influential in spreading the laurels of your library. Opinion makers work with many people, talk with them, serve them, form their attitudes. They may be a major asset to librarians. Here are some opinion makers to know:

PUBLIC LIBRARIES

City Council members
Mayor
Chief of police
Newspaper editor
Barbers and beauty operators
Radio and TV directors
Insurance agents
Chamber of Commerce
  members
Cab drivers

City Manager
Mail carriers
Doctors
Clergy
Employment-service personnel
Travel agents
Recreation directors
Richest person in town
Municipal judges
Attorneys

SCHOOL LIBRARIES

Secretary to principal
Principal
Vice-principal
Coach
Sports stars

Counselor
President of school board
Personnel manager
Head of receiving department
Nurse

Honor students   Senior teacher on staff
President of PTA   Cub Scout Den Mothers
Class political leaders   Boy Scoutmasters
Psychologist   Superintendent of schools

COLLEGE AND UNIVERSITY LIBRARIES

Secretaries   Personnel Manager
Vice-president   Campus barber
President   Student debate-team members
Expediter   Radicals
Director of public relations   Program manager of radio
President of married-students   station
   association   Graduate placement advisor
Best-liked professor   Head of maintenance
Most-honored professor   Registrar
Student-body president   Drama students
Editor of campus newspaper   Board of Regents
Student sports stars

SPECIAL LIBRARIES

Receptionist   President
Vice-presidents   Secretaries
Personnel Manager   Guard
Head Accountant   Mailroom clerks
Expediter   Stenographers
Messengers   Director of public relations

Opinion makers lay the foundation of support and change for your library, but public opinion may also move in an opposite direction. The climate of what people in your community think of your program and service is largely up to you. How well you work at generating a favorable response through both your good service and your relationship with opinion makers helps determine the future of your library.

Action Makers

Opinion makers fashion the setting. Action makers initiate the concrete changes. Without the favor of action makers big changes in policy or personnel or construction are difficult uphill battles. These people are the ones who decide policy.

They're the handlers of money, the creators of positions, the managers of administrative units. They are usually the ones who have the final word on increases of expenditures or the acquisitions of a large controversial collection or the broadening of service that requires additional professional positions.

Know who your local action makers are. Better yet, know them face to face and name to name. If you don't, they may make remote decisions on your unit without the slightest concern about how these decisions affect your working program. Force them, by knowing them, to make decisions affecting your library that take into account the living, breathing, frustrated personnel rather than merely an inanimate library unit. Saying "No" to a professional friend is much more difficult than to a professional function.

Here are some action makers to know:

City Council members	Boards
Executive assistants	Vice-presidents
Comptrollers	Bankers
Managers	Newsmen and women
Supervisors	Lobbyists
Presidents	Business managers
Directors	Legislators
Principals	

Legislators

Opinion makers and action makers are Very Important People. They make your library go round. Of all of them, probably the ones who have the power for momentous, long-range influence on your library are legislators. Municipal, county, borough, state, and federal legislators work for their constituency, the people who support them and whom they represent. Legislators are the great and relatively untapped source of energy and wealth librarians need to mine.

A Machiavellian attitude librarians might adopt toward legislators is not as heinous as it sounds. On the other hand, it's not as virtuous as operating the library store and hoping for the best. Niccolò Machiavelli wrote *The Prince* in 1532 as a practical guide to political power. The book is filled with shocking reminders of how political power and influence are gained in the world about us. Machiavelli was no demon, but he did write about some of the demonic devices of political and social behavior.

Machiavelli shamelessly wrote such Olympian insights as "for how we live is no different from how we ought to live." He knew that a prince or someone in power or authority need not be virtuous or competent but merely must appear so. He saw that those who got ahead on the financial and status ladders included those who were more bold than cautious.

Politics

Librarians need not subscribe to all the horrors of *The Prince.* Yet for their own benefit they should be aware that a vast network of persuasion, political give-and-take, under-the-table swappings of advantages, pressures of friendships and allegiances, promotion of special interests, and other behind-the-scenes activities exist long before any kind of vote or action is taken on the public legislative floors.

You as a professional librarian must get involved in politics at any level. Learn by experience how your princes arrive at decisions that relate to your cherished profession. You can't expect to win all the political battles. If you don't get involved in some of them, you'll win hardly any. Politicians don't vote for issues they don't care about or if they have no direct responsibility to the backers of those issues.

Librarians have for too long used the white-cane-and-tin-cup approach to legislators in order to get what they want. Unfortunately, this approach usually yields pennies instead of silver dollars. Librarians (librarians think) are nice people, and legislators will do nice things for them. Justice will prevail. Good will be recognized.

Look to the Future

The sentiment that librarians will be rewarded is appropriate, but the method isn't. Just as librarians should know other opinion makers and action makers, so should they know legislators. Once legislators know librarians they will feel more responsibility to them. The sophisticated technique is to work to elect future legislators. This means getting in the habit of looking toward tomorrow, not yesterday. Determine which candidates for office are your friends. Get to know them personally, and get to know them early in their campaigns. Support them for office. Go to their coffees and teas. Talk with them at their headquarters. Meet with their campaign manager. Offer to help in the campaign chore of addressing envelopes or writing statements or, better yet, offering reference service and information for campaign speeches. March behind their campaigns at the beginning of the game, not merely the day before election. Realize that a legislator librarians did not help elect is not going to be converted easily to thinking libraries.

Don't expect your princes to be perfect. Do expect them to know you. Even then, all your legislators won't share your heartfelt aspirations that development of libraries is important for the advancement of humankind. Legislators come from the people's ranks. They are truck drivers, fishermen, contractors, wholesalers, and shopkeepers, as well as lawyers and university professors. Some of them will figure that the expansion of library services has a priority of nineteen on a list of eighteen. You have to be prepared for the legislator who "don't put no faith in books nohow."

Remember that politics operates on the iceberg theory. What is out in public view is only a minor part compared with what is really going on behind the scenes. Librarians must establish the support of the chairperson of whatever committee is dealing with their bills or interests. They must especially have a connecting line to the finance and rules committees, two of the most important in state and federal legislatures.

Competition is the name of the political game at all levels. The way librarians meet this competition determines their future program. Look to the future. Scratch a legislator's back early enough and the legislator will scratch yours later on.

City Councils

Attend City Council meetings. Examine firsthand the process of how community tax money is portioned out and

whether there is an appropriate and speedy follow-up of the
budget. Talk with the Council members during recesses, before
and after meetings. Let them know you are interested in how
they conduct themselves on the floor and that you are watching
closely what they will do with the issues of education, especially
those concerning libraries. Keep them on their toes. If you
don't, merchants, school parents, real-estate owners, used-car
dealers, and others with special interests will.

Legislative Reporting

Legislators at a higher level are more difficult to watch. This
stops too many people. Don't let it stop you. Both state and
federal governments have legislative reporting services that
provide copies of each bill submitted to the floor and periodic
summaries of the action, if any, taken on these bills. Some
librarians thumb through the stack of bills as soon as they
arrive in the receiving department in order to find any and all
bills that are related to libraries. More librarians should do so.
This procedure can keep all local librarians aware and up-to-
date on friendly legislators who introduced library-related
bills, those who voted for their passage, and those who are
likely to support future library-related bills.

Knowing who their friends are in the legislatures, librarians
can build a current list of addresses and committee assignments of these good guys. With such a card file handy,
librarians can quickly write letters to legislators when certain
bills need to be brought to the forefront, or may send
telegrams when a bill is brought to the floor for a vote.

The important part is to establish a structure of communication, no matter how small it is:

• Keep an accurate card file of addresses of legislators.

• During legislative sessions maintain a routine of thumbing
through copies of bills as they arrive at the library.

• Make periodic checks of legislative reporting services.

• Have brief forms ready to send to local librarians to suggest
they write one particular legislator about one particular bill.

• Set up practical procedures for reacting quickly by sending telegrams to legislators when an important bill suddenly comes to the floor for voting.

• Keep stamps, envelopes, and letterhead stationery available for the sole purpose of contacting legislators.

Library Associations

One of the necessary tools to use in order to profit from legislative action is a strong state library organization. Communication within the state association must be clear and fast. The legislative committee of an association must be chaired by a doer, someone who reacts quickly to the quick change of events in government. Newsletters should be flexible enough so that extra issues regarding unexpected legislative action may be published; these must include the latest bills about to be voted upon.

Politics is a network game. No one gets elected from an island. Similarly, librarians, with their special interest in libraries, must build their own network if they wish to be effective. No library-related bill gets passed, let alone introduced, without such effort.

The American Association of School Librarians is an example of a national legislative network. State chairpeople are notified of impending library-related bills in Washington, D.C., and, representing their state organizations, they either write letters to key legislators or mobilize other local librarians to do the same. The California Association of School Librarians is an example of a state organization with its own legislative network. More such organizations are needed across the country.

Lobbyists

A large library association may also be strong enough to finance a professional lobbyist at the state capital, as the American Library Association does at the national level in Washington, D.C. State associations with smaller treasuries may have to rely on the state librarian in the capital city to lobby on behalf of library bills.

Another alternative is for a state association to hire "half a lobbyist," that is, share a lobbyist with another profession. The standard arrangement for state associations is to establish a split-assignment with one of the lobbyists for the education profession. An arrangement may be made for a lobbyist to use half the time for education and half for library issues. Possibly an arrangement could be made to have a representative of the library profession on hand for consultation with legislators rather than developing an aggressive lobbying situation. A lobbyist's salary would be commensurate with the arrangement.

Lobbyists are often termed the "Third House" of government. Their name is derived from the entrance halls of capitol buildings, where the general public would wait to talk with legislators and to make requests for passage or defeat of certain bills. Some states require registration of all lobbyists and information concerning what organizations or professions employ them and the amount of their salaries.

Lobbyists for libraries can be effective. Traditionally lobbyists provide information and background material to legislators about matters relating to their interests. When a legislator does not have time to research the per capita expenditures of existing libraries in outlying areas of a state, the legislator may ask a lobbyist to provide this information or other data that would be helpful in assessing reasons for or against the passage of a bill.

The members of the "Third House" have been criticized for giving highly selective statistics, background material, and explanation of situations. Much of the lobbyist's work has been considered distorted and overly concerned with special interests rather than the general public interest. Nearly every legislator, however, agrees that lobbyists not only provide an outlet for the people to petition the government, a right guaranteed under the First Amendment of the Constitution, but that they also help legislators immensely in assisting government to act upon measures with some basis of information rather than conjecture. Many legislators suggest that lobbyists are essential to the proper functioning of republican government.

Unfortunately, librarians who view lobbyists for the library profession as essential are few and far between. Perhaps this is one reason that the per capita proportion of legislative budgets for library service is so low compared with pork-barrel construction of highways, tax benefits for oil companies, farm subsidies, and other big lobbyist interests.

The Legislative Process

Our government is so fundamentally structured to the grass roots that any individual in a community may introduce a bill into the legislature through legislators. The normal course of events is for individuals to present ideas and draft a measure in outline form for presentation to a legislator first. Then a legislator either puts the individual's proposed bill into the proper legislative format or submits it to a legislative-affairs agency, which in turn drafts the bill in the correct technical terms and form.

After the bill is introduced into the legislative mill, it passes through an intricate system of checks and counter-checks before final approval and passage. The vast majority of bills introduced never find the way out of this maze. A bill may be stopped as a result of political bickering, inaction, stupidity, or sacrifice for a greater public good, or it may be derailed by trickery, superseded by another similar but better bill, or amended *ad infinitum* until it becomes unrecognizable. Proposed funds may gradually be eliminated until the bill becomes gutless, or it may simply be a bad one to begin with. Whatever the reason, the odds are great against any bill, even one related to libraries, progressing through the legislative process unscathed and unamended.

Nevertheless, librarians who wish to become more involved in political activity, because they know that is where the money is ultimately allocated for some of their programs, should know the precarious path a bill takes on its way to passage. here is the standard legislative labyrinth:

• A particular bill is introduced in (for example) the House for consideration by all legislators.

- Bill is recorded by the Chief Clerk.

- Speaker of the House assigns it to a committee (Finance, Judiciary, Education, Welfare, etc.) for examination and recommendation for further action.

- Committee considers the bill by deliberating its merits and demerits.

- Bill goes out of committee and to the floor of the legislature for general debate, for amendment, for passage by vote, or for return to committee.

- If the bill passes, the Speaker signs it.

- Chief Clerk signs it.

- Bill is sent to the Senate.

- Secretary of the Senate reads the bill by title.

- President of the Senate assigns it to committee for consideration.

- Committee considers merits and demerits of the bill.

- Bill comes out of committee and moves to the floor for public debate, amendment, passage, or return to committee.

- If the bill passes the vote, the President of the Senate signs it.

- Secretary of the Senate signs it.

- Bill is returned to the House.

- Record is made of the Senate message concerning the action of the bill.

- Bill is signed by the Speaker of the House.

- Signed by the Chief Clerk of the House.

- Signed again by the President of the Senate and Secretary of the Senate.

- Recorded and returned to the House.

- Speaker of the House orders that the bill be transmitted to the Governor.

- Bill is either signed or vetoed by the Governor.

- Bill is filed with the Secretary of State.

- The passed bill is then sent to the Legislative Affairs Agency to be included in the State Statutes as law.

A Network, Not a Tightrope

When it comes to matters of money, the importance of Very Important People cannot be overstated. Opinion makers and action makers are the people who allow you to build a library program to serve all the people all the time. Without their support in one form or another, your library will probably remain at the status quo while other institutions in society step forward with the times.

In the last analysis, it is usually better to do what you are best at. As a librarian you should be best at providing library service. Probably nothing would be more impressive to opinion makers and action makers than deluging them personally with library service so courteous, so reliable, so accurate, so truly helpful, time-saving, and excellent, as to completely mystify them as to how you can perform so well with such meager resources and facilities. If a principal wishes aloud that he could at least read a review of a book since no time is left to read the book itself, don't complain that books are being short-changed. Satisfy the need and rush a review to the office. If a scientist mentions in passing that it's difficult to find the latest evaluation of moon-rock tektites, rush the latest evaluations into her hands.

Nothing impresses people so much in this day and age of mass shoddiness as a job well done. Nothing startles so much as service over and above the call of the job description. All this takes work and effort and breeds its own frustration. However, if more librarians borrowed some of the more acceptable tenets of Machiavelli, if more of them worked at threading together a system of public support and interest, of looking to the legislative future, of cashing in on campaign support, and of cultivating the loyalties of decision makers, then perhaps future legislation will vastly improve upon the present economics of libraries. After all, it is far easier to walk a network than a tightrope.

15 Evaluating Your Public Relations Program

All library programs should be evaluated periodically for their effectiveness. Your public relations program is no exception. Some kind of self-evaluation, even if it is cursory, is necessary for your continued public relations success. This is a basic but too-often-neglected part of any such program.

Self-Criticism Generates Progress

Professional advertising agencies face trouble in accurately measuring their results in direct relation to their efforts, and they have the money for elaborate polls and surveys. They do know, however, as should you, that self-criticism generates progress. If your public relations program is to be effective and to progress, be certain to take the time to evaluate what you are doing, so that you may both plan for the future and correct mistakes of the past. Even a somewhat casual look at your program may indicate general trends and give you confidence in creating additions and improvements.

If it is to be valuable, evaluation should be carried out as your public relations program moves along, not merely after all is said and done. Five methods can be used in your evaluation: 1) study the needs of your particular library; 2) collate media outlets; 3) pretest public relations materials; 4) determine media response; 5) compile people response.

All five are interrelated, but the last is the most important in terms of public relations goals themselves and the one to which the others lead.

Study the Needs of Your Library

Too often librarians become so immersed in day-to-day routine that they find little time to sit back and look at the general direction the library is headed. Librarians must take this time. It is important.

Establishing goal priorities can refresh the spirit of a library and generate a deeper involvement of a staff by letting them know how they fit into the complex. Staff members should know in which way they contribute to the library movement toward better service. They can't participate if they don't know where or what is the finish line.

Ask yourself some overview questions of your library:

- Is your library keeping up with trends in the profession?

- Is your library taking advantage of a systems approach to planning?

- Does your library make a continual effort to invite people inside, or does it merely wait for them?

- Do you feel you are currently serving enough people?

- Is your library aware of the current needs of your service area?

- Does your library merely act on the premises it always did in the past?

- Does the working atmosphere in your library stretch the talents of the staff to full potential?

- Does your library anticipate the needs of your community by providing services and programs before crises arise?

Questions like these force answers that take overall goals into account. Just as you must decide beforehand the purpose for which you are making a film or writing a news release or inaugurating a story hour, so must you be consciously aware of your general public relations goals. Knowing the big picture makes it easier to fit all the smaller pieces together.

Once overall goals are clear, then the need to publicize them internally and externally becomes apparent. Goals are useless unless more than the select group that runs the show knows about them. Decide how to publicize your program goals:

- How often do you schedule general staff meetings?

- Do you distribute the meeting minutes to the public?

- Is the local newspaper sufficient for publicity?

- How many radio stations are there in town? What are their rates? Would they provide public-service time?

- How much would a newsletter cost? Who would edit it? What should it contain? Editorials?

- Should a speaking circuit be organized?

- Should displays be set up in public places? Posters in store windows?

- Would a film be feasible? Or a slide presentation?

Collate Media Outlets

Knowing the communication channels through which your public relations materials are distributed is important both in measuring their anticipated audience and in deciding how they should be prepared. The great time and effort necessary to produce such material demand planning, not only of the content but also of the selection of the most appropriate and effective media outlets.

Put a leash around some of your ideas so that your public relations program has direction and long-range cumulative success. Material good for newspapers is not necessarily good for television. What is appropriate for radio is not necessarily appropriate for displays. In other words, evaluate your media outlets in terms of media format, audience anticipated, time schedules, durability, re-use, educational level. Know at the outset where you are headed with your material. This helps reduce revision and focuses your energy on development of material totally in tune with the particular communication channel you select.

Collating your media outlets also provides you with a blanket program. Take pencil and paper and list possible outlets along with their apparent effectiveness and cost. Include everything from television to single-page handouts. This concrete list in effect tells you that all publicity does not have to go into newspapers. Rather, certain information is best handled by mail, other information by airport displays. Tabulate the field of media outlets in ratio to your needs and their effectiveness. You'll save money as well as reach the right people at the right time.

Ask some of these questions of your possible outlets:

- What is the circulation of the local newspaper in relation to the city population?

- Morning or evening paper? (Morning papers generally have more hard news, evening more features.)

- What are the educational levels of local radio and television audiences?

- Where are there constant crowds of people?

- At what time of day is a particular medium most effective?

- How much are the production and mailing costs of a newsletter? flyer? postcards?

- What medium would reach the most people? the least? the most influential? the elite? the poor?

- What medium may be redistributed? has the longest life? the shortest?

- Are all the inexpensive media automatically the least effective?

- Which one is the easiest for you to produce for?

Pretest Public Relations Material

Don't take for granted that whatever your produce in the way of publicity packages will somehow all be understood and appreciated. Take time to examine carefully your news releases and displays and the other material designed and intended for the public eye. You may catch a glaring error that, if released, might be damaging.

If time permits, put your materials away for a day or two. Then return to them with a critical eye. A breather time often produces a more objective outlook and lessens your possessive adherence to your creation, even if it's bad or inaccurate or inappropriate.

Better yet, take your products to a few outsiders to have them examined critically. Let these outsiders take their time. Don't lead them on. Simply ask them, "What does this mean to you? Do you understand all of it?"

Members of your staff are not the persons to ask. Your public relations materials are aimed toward the people you serve: the public should be asked. If people mention that they do not understand a certain phrase, you can change it before it gets to a larger audience and more people fail to understand it. Don't use professional jargon. You must not assume that a layperson knows what a main catalog entry is or understands other fundamental aspects of library procedure.

Check, too, to be certain that your wording is absolutely understandable. Simple words, simple sentences, and simple paragraphs with concrete and personal references are essential to the understanding of what you produce. Remember: use words to express, not impress.

Before general public release ask yourself some of these questions:

- Is every word clear and understandable?

- Do the pictures tell the story clearly and simply?

- Are all fundamental steps of the particular story explained for the layperson?

- Is all professional jargon removed?

- Is the main point you wish to convey to an audience actually conveyed?

- Is audience interest held until the end of the material?

- Are the contents, structure, and format appropriate to the intended medium of communication?

- What aspect is superfluous and may be eliminated?

- What needs to be added to make the material absolutely clear?

- Does the material create an impact or inspire a shrug?

Determine Media Response

A solid measure of whether your material meets professional standards is its use by newspaper editors or program directors of radio and television stations. If they do use it, then you've met their demands in format and content. If not, then either your material did not meet their standards or other material was given priority because of time factors, news importance, or pure personal prejudice.

The manager of an office building may comment on the attractiveness of your display and mention that many people stop to look at it. This positive reaction is not something you should take lightly. Such comments mean that you have succeeded with this particular medium of communication. Professional graphic artists may compliment you on a display or take interest in your ideas. If you get such a reaction, you've succeeded. A manager of another governmental agency may comment on the effectiveness of a newsletter you send through her office. Or a newspaper editor may pick up an item from a newsletter and print it in his paper. Again you've succeeded.

Such professional reaction indicates how you're meeting the competition of public display. No matter how friendly you are with a newspaper editor or a story manager, they cannot afford to use inept material. Such professionals are good gauges of the general public reaction, since their business is to know and to anticipate what will appeal and be absorbed by their audiences.

To help determine their effectiveness, ask these questions about your promotional material:

- Did the media use the material you submitted?

- How did they use it? Buried on a back page? After the midnight movie rerun?

- Was the material changed? a little? drastically?

- Was some material not used for identifiable political or social reasons? Some you may eliminate in the future?

- Is the editor or program director receptive to library publicity in general?

- Any comment after the material appeared in the media?

- Did the professionals compliment you on your presentation of the material?

- Did they mention they would like similar material in the future? If not, do you get this positive feeling?

Compile People Response

One of the primary purposes of public relations is to persuade your current and potential patrons to explore and use your library. Yet all the public relations material you generate doesn't in itself tell you what response, if any, you created. A deliberate attempt should be made to ascertain in some way what this response amounts to.

Without the ways and means of a staff of pollsters and in-depth surveyors, librarians must be satisfied with less formal and involved findings. These are likely to be less accurate, but they provide you with general trends, indications of the tide of public feelings, and whether or not your public relations work is making headway.

Some libraries already keep elaborate statistics and records. Unfortunately, chances are that they do not keep them with public relations goals in mind. They should. Those in charge of public relations programs owe it to themselves, and their superiors should get periodic reports on effectiveness.

Librarians should keep a public relations scrapbook or

folder of newspaper clippings and pictures, notes on radio and television broadcasts, and displays, copies of pamphlets, bookmarks, book lists, and newsletters, and all other public relations creations. Such a scrapbook pulls together in a concrete record of work that may be referred to at any time.

One surefire way of gathering people response is simply to ask direct questions: "Would you send your children to a story hour on Saturday afternoon?" "What do you think of the new library building proposed in the newspaper yesterday?" "Did you find that new display interesting?"

Move around among patrons. Strike up conversations to get to know their interests and reactions to library procedures. They are the ones you serve. The better you know them the better you may serve them.

Pay attention to complaints in letters, on the telephone, and at the front desk. A single complaint doesn't necessarily indicate an isolated case. It may spotlight a service that needs to be reconsidered. Television networks, for example, figure that one letter represents 1,000 other people who have similar feelings but do not write. The same iceberg theory, though perhaps not in the same large numbers, works for libraries as well.

Statistics offer a valuable means of before-and-after comparisons. Fortunately, the library world has a tradition of statistical record keeping, although there is a trend toward doing away with many library statistics at a time when such records are becoming increasingly widespread in other professions in this computer age. Statistics may be used in promotional packages as well as in annual reports to justify budget increases. They also give day-to-day tallies of work load and may help the supervisors and managers who every day grow more needful of job justification and efficiency. Prepare for the management consultant.

Nearly all libraries keep records in the three basic areas of acquisitions, cataloging, and circulation. These statistics usually include books, periodicals, videotapes, records, and other material circulated, and volumes added, volumes weeded. However, limiting records at this point fails to take account of many uses of the library other than checking out books and returning them.

Answering reference questions, no matter on what level, is an extremely important service. Some sort of record should be kept to indicate whether responses to your invitation to use library resources are increasing or decreasing. Simply because it is difficult to measure the quality of reference service doesn't mean you shouldn't try. Besides, a record of reference questions furnishes you with concrete information about what reference librarians do all day, information that can justify the positions; spotlights trends of user interest; supplies means of gauging what reference books to purchase; leaves a legacy for new members of a reference staff to ponder; and gives a written source of the more unusual and humorous questions asked, to exploit for public relations purposes.

Reference statistical sheets can't cover everything, but here is one form that takes only about fifteen seconds to complete after each question:

| | | Time | | | | | |
Date	Subject (source)	0–5	5–10	10–	Direc-tional	Tele-phone	Letter
9–3	Alpha backscattering (*Scientific Am.*)			X			X
"	Size of Senegal (*World Almanac*)	X				X	

Two other important statistical records that show user response are door counts and body counts at various hours of the day. Circulation records do not reveal the number of people who use a library without charging out material. Many people go into a library to study, to read newspapers and periodicals, to browse through reserve books and material in special collections, to read open-shelf books without borrowing them, to sit and think.

A body count at a library entrance provides valuable indications of patron use. Department-store managers, government officials, traffic controllers, and others find information of this type useful in evaluating and planning their own services. So would librarians.

Student workers can move through a library to count the number of people during certain periods of the day. The results over a length of time yield charts of information helpful in staffing a library, anticipating the influx of patrons, and measuring the effects of any promotional programs geared to specific hours of the day.

Keep records of telephone calls to the circulation desk and to administrators. Any response of the people to your library should be recorded briefly in some way. Together, such records give you a somewhat comprehensive analysis of how your library with its many resources performs in relation to the people of your service area.

Ask some of these questions of the people response to your public relations materials:

- Has anyone volunteered comments on what they saw or heard of the library?

- Did a particular piece of public relations material temporarily attract an unusual number of people?

- Do your records show an upswing in library use since your rejuvenated public relations program started?

- Have you received complaints about any area of your program?

- Has the library staff noticed a changed atmosphere since your public relations materials have taken hold?

- Do patrons seem to use certain library facilities and materials not used before?

- Has any outsider said, "Gee, I didn't know you had that here? I saw it in the paper."

These five methods of evaluating your public relations program should be used as each aspect of your program progresses from planning to execution. Communication involves a multitude of factors. Distribution of material is only one factor. Getting an article in a newspaper doesn't necessarily mean that it will be read. Readability, placement on the page, attitudes and educational background of the reader, time of day, and other factors all influence potential impact of an article.

Evaluation makes it far easier to set up further plans; the record of past successes and failures allows you to know what to correct and what to repeat.

Self-evaluation is always difficult both to implement and to accept. Not the least difficult is remembering that increased patron use of your library may have resulted from something other than better public relations. What comes *after* does not necessarily mean *as a result of*. Nevertheless, you won't worry about this when someone comes up and says, "I'll say this, things are sure perking up in this library."

16 Developing a Continuing Program

A few successes in library publicity do not equal a successful library public relations program. A photo in a newspaper one month, a mention of National Library Week on radio the next month, are gratifying achievements. They represent hard work and enthusiasm, but what happens next? Will anything happen next?

A Program, Not Piecemeal

To ensure that public relations material continues to be produced and to appear in the public, a sound *program* must be developed. Without a structured, officially sanctioned program, your public relations work soon deteriorates into hit-or-miss publicity attempts reluctantly put together by someone on off-hours, done in a hurry, and quickly doomed to become drudgery once the spirit of dedication wears thin. Library public relations cannot rest on the waxing and waning of general staff interest. Such attempts surely end up unbalanced and short-lived.

Firm commitment to a public relations program, not helter skelter publicity, is the primary ingredient for long-range success. Public relations programs in libraries, probably more than any other program, need such commitment if for no other reason than because extremely few formal programs exist around the country. A casual affirmation that yes-publicizing-a-library-would-be-a-nice-thing is not enough.

You must be convinced that a comprehensive attempt to reach more people demands a strong pledge of action. Nothing short of this ever forms the base of a good public relations program. It never has and never will.

A *Public Relations Position*

One example of concrete evidence of such a commitment is to create a position or to assign someone already on a staff to promote a library, preferably on a full-time basis. In most cases libraries will be financially unable to make such a drastic move immediately. A library may not be large enough, or because of related programs already in effect such a position may not be required. Working toward such a goal, however, is vital.

If a full-time person is not feasible, then time must be set aside during the day for a librarian to work on public relations projects. The time should be explicitly designated for planning and executing news releases, coordinating library displays, drafting bibliographies, working with other librarians in a community to synchronize approaches for optimum effectiveness, and for other related activities.

The rest of the library staff should know that time has been officially set aside for this individual to work on public relations and that their suggestions or help would be appreciated. The entire staff should be encouraged to take an interest in widening the perspective of their library and to realize that their concern and enthusiasm in all that they do should be for the ultimate benefit of current and potential library patrons.

The clear assignment of someone to work in an official capacity on public relations, even if only for one day or a half-day of the week, is essential. Without this commitment of personnel, no public relations program will last for long.

Year-Long Planning

Once someone is in fact your official public relations staff member, this person can establish a fundamental structure for the public relations program. If you are this person, then you must think in somewhat larger terms than merely what to do next for a community newspaper.

One way to structure your program is to take a year's calendar and carefully thumb through it. Jot down on a piece of paper the seasons and key holidays so that they are all before you at a glance. You might search *Chases' Calender of Annual Events,* which lists may offbeat daily, weekly, and monthly celebrations. The Chamber of Commerce may have a list of celebrations that are specifically appropriate to your own community.

This exercise gives you a spectrum of an entire year in terms of what and how your library might help a community celebrate. Such a list provides you with enough advance time to prepare material with care rather than in a rush. For example, in July you might begin to plan and produce an attractive list of books including information on unusual ways of cooking a Thanksgiving turkey.

By setting up a year-long program you coordinate your time and effort better. Your work load is spread more evenly, and your materials improve as a result. In addition, you can cope more easily with sudden last-minute projects and yet keep many other projects in the mill at the same time.

List Deadlines

Decide how you wish to space out your calendar of public relations events. Your personal timetable is the first step toward mustering these projects out of your head and into concrete action. A deadline pushes people forward like nothing else. You may not meet all your self-imposed deadlines, but without some sort of written schedule you may well not meet any of them.

Allot Time

You must decide, too, how much time to allot each project. This depends on the time granted you for public relations work as a whole. How much time you are given determines whether or not you can produce a library newsletter once a month or only quarterly, book lists for every major season or only for key holidays, displays in some of the town shops or only at your library, talks on radio and television or only at a few women's clubs. The important consideration is to parcel out your time as accurately as possible within the context of an entire year. This kind of preliminary scheduling yields the best use of your time and gives you a platform from which to begin.

Twelve-Month File Folders

A file of twelve manila folders, one for the projects for each month, helps organize your program at the outset. Label each folder with an individual month. Then use each folder to assemble research material for one or two or a dozen major projects you have planned for this particular month.

For example, for June the library may plan a summer reading program for children or adults. During the year you may run across unusual titles that would be especially attractive to your community. Before you forget, write down the titles and call numbers on a piece of paper and put them into the June folder. Perhaps you may run across some interesting biographical information about authors included in the reading program. Slip this information into the folder for retrieval later when you actually begin the program promotion. By then the June folder will contain bits and pieces of references that will make it far easier to plan the project. You'll have concrete material and ideas to set your imagination whirling.

Idea File

You should also maintain an idea file: nearly all public relations professionals do. It may include anything that strikes your fancy. Photocopy an unusual magazine advertisement for speed-reading and slip it into your file for future reference. Jot down any catchy phrase you hear on the radio and file it away for rainy days. An unlikely but effective combination of objects in a department-store window may be especially appealing. Make a note of the display and how it might relate to libraries. Then include it in your idea file. Company brochures with striking layout designs offer innumerable possibilities for solving your own design problems. File these brochures away for the future.

Once you become aware of public relations materials in

newspapers, magazines, radio, television, store windows, billboards, neon lights, political campaigns, food packaging, colorful signs, and the other outlets, get in the habit of saving the material or making notes for your idea file. Borrowing the gist of someone else's good idea and then applying it to your own projects saves you time and consternation. If you steal from one source, you're plagiarizing; if you steal from multiple sources, you're researching. Don't plagiarize.

Name-and-Address File

Another foundation block for your continuing promotion program is a file of names and addresses on 3" × 5" cards. Gather names and addresses of key media personnel or anyone who might be a source for you to contact in placing public relations materials. These people may include editors of newspapers, program directors of radio and television stations, printers, graphic artists, local historians, local writers, library trustees, school-board members, public relations representatives of local companies, City Council members, the Mayor, other librarians in the area—in short, anyone who could be helpful in your projects.

Take the time to set up your own name-and-address file even if it overlaps the telephone book. Try to establish a certain autonomy of operations in your public relations work. By having your own idea file, your own address file, your own schedule of proposed projects, you confirm an official commitment for increased and concerned library promotion. Being as professional in method as you can often brings forth professionalism in a final product.

The reinforcement of your commitment to a program of library promotion must be approached from all possible angles. The tradition of the library profession has been to play down, if not ignore, efforts to reach out to individuals who are not apparently interested in a library. This tradition is difficult to overcome. To do so demands not only persuading the layperson that librarians are serious about bringing more people into a library but also persuading many *librarians* that this is necessary and desirable.

Public Relations in the Budget

Many libraries find problems in justifying recognition of an officially constituted, aggressive promotion program. Yet if such a program is to have any hope of survival, it must be recognized in the general library budget, no matter how minimally and no matter how buried (initially) among other priorities.

Your public relations program may be represented in a budget as an explicit line item or may be hidden behind terminological opulence. Whatever you do, get it in the ledger. A public relations program must be considered a vital segment of an overall library program of service. All the talk about reaching out to the people, about aggressively inviting them into your distribution house of informational and recreational materials, about committing your library to modern public relations techniques, is utterly vacuous without some basic budgetary assignment. Where there's a will there's a wallet.

A library wallet for public relations may be slim at the beginning, but it will fatten if your program has merit and provides an informing service that in turn enlarges the scope of your overall services.

Your own separate record of library public relations work provides you with ammunition to increase a budget. This is when your scrapbook of public relations efforts become valuable. This is the time when your before-and-after statistics have relevance and your surveys and interviews show results. You know then that good public relations produces increased recognition and use of a library, as your files show. And better public relations could produce better results—if only increased funds were available.

Ultimately, however, the central thread of a continuing program is *you*. You are the core. Your qualities of self-discipline, sustained enthusiasm, insight into the profession, and an excellence in spreading the good word for what your library has to offer, all form a special energetic network of personal interest that sets a public relations program solidly in tune with the times and, even more importantly, in tune with your particular community.

17 Case Study of Cooperation for Library Promotion

A small group of public, school, university, and special librarians in Fairbanks, Alaska, showed what could be done in a small way in library promotion when they all got together to pool their talents and resources. For more than a year all library publicity in the town was directed toward the run-down, understaffed, underspaced, pre-oil boom, log-cabin public library. The simple long-range goal was to build community interest in the public library, with the hope that the townspeople would see what the library could be and wasn't and that they would therefore be more inclined to support a bond issue for a new building.

Log-Cabin Library

The oil rush on the North Slope of Alaska channeled a great deal of nationwide attention to Fairbanks, but the community itself changed little in actual fact. The Fairbanks area had a population of approximately 40,000 people. A borough county-like government for an area of more than 7,000 square miles had within its jurisdiction a public library.

The library was built of logs in 1906, and looked it. The book collection totaled about 18,000 volumes (not titles). Seating space disappeared after less than a dozen patrons came through the sagging doorway. Space for administration and processing of books made hunchbacks of the staff.

Extraordinary Spirit

On the other hand, the spirit of local librarians was extraordinary. A small group of them, the ones who attended all the local chapter meetings of the Alaska Library Association, decided to gear themselves toward concerted action. They pledged continuing promotional support for the public library as the central project of the local chapter for the year. They established committees and outlined publicity projects, large and small. The seemingly insignificant projects were considered just as important as the big splashy ones in the achievement of the overall goal.

The principal objective was to encourage as many townspeople as possible to visit the public library and thereby see firsthand its deplorable condition. The campaign worked. Here's what these half-dozen Fairbanks librarians did:

Radio Book Reviews

Five librarians arranged with the program manager of radio station KUAC-FM at the University of Alaska to produce book reviews, each two-and-a-half minutes long. Each librarian selected a different field: best-seller fiction, nonfiction, children's books, homemaking books, technical books for the layperson. Each librarian wrote and narrated one review a week. The tape for the week was distributed to sixteen stations around the state. More importantly, "Bookslot," as it was called, was played on KUAC twice a day, and on a regularly scheduled 10:20 a.m. program on one of the two local commercial stations in town. All the books reviewed were taken from the new-book shelf of the Fairbanks Public Library. Each reviewer stated at the conclusion of the review something like: "This and other fascinating books are available at the Fairbanks Public Library. Visit it soon."

Newspaper Photo Features

Another committee produced picture spreads on the many different kinds of libraries in Fairbanks, showing how they related to the public library. These were published in both the *Fairbanks Daily News-Miner* and *Jessen's Daily,* as were action shots of children in the crowded children's room at the public library. Also printed were single shots of the head librarian receiving special donations to the library, photos of distinguished visitors or special meetings, and a series featuring librarians in the community.

Book Column

A University of Alaska librarian wrote a weekly book-review column for the Sunday edition of *Jessen's Daily.* "Bookline" reviewed titles taken from the public library's shelves. The writer emphasized the fact frequently, thereby bringing more notice to the local library.

Letters to Legislators

A special librarian at Fort Wainwright Army Base near Fairbanks organized a rotating system of letter writing to local legislators. Each month librarians in the local chapter were given the names and addresses of legislators to write to about the library budget, upgrading of the entire educational program, requests for federal funds for library construction, and other issues in the news.

Civic Leaders at Library Meetings

The program chairwoman for the local chapter invited community officials to exchange views on library problems and potentials. The borough chairman was invited one month, a member of the state House of Representatives the next. All the local state legislators were invited to the annual banquet, and nearly all attended.

ALA Film and Radio Clips

The public librarian arranged for funds to purchase the American Library Association 16mm thirty-second color sound films and short radio messages designed for general library promotion. Intended primarily for National Library Week, the films and radio clips were produced without a time tie-in so that they could be used throughout the year. The librarian distributed them to the local movie theater, the two television stations, and the three radio stations in town. The clips were played periodically throughout the year, as planned.

Exhibits

Two librarians set up at the Fairbanks International Airport an exhibit of best-sellers of the twentieth century, the books being taken from the public library and labeled so. The occasion was National Library Week, and the display attracted many passengers. Smaller exhibits were set up in the public library itself, including a listing of the books that were being reviewed that week on the "Bookslot" radio program.

Book Lists Distributed

For the 1967 centennial of the purchase of Alaska from Russia, an Alaska Library Association committee published a book list of Alaskana. The list was illustrated, annotated, and printed attractively. After the celebration the remaining copies of the list were available to any library in the state. Fairbanks librarians ordered 5,000 and placed packets of them for distribution at hotels and motels, travel agencies, tour bureaus, the bookstore, and select general merchandise stores in town. The lists were offered with the compliments of the public library, where most of the titles were available.

Time-of-Day Message

The public librarian recorded a five-second message on a special tape recorder at the local telephone company. Every time a caller dialed for the time of day came: "The North Star Borough Public Library is on the move. Visit it soon."

Attendance at Municipal Meetings

The public librarian and many other librarians attended as many city and borough council meetings as possible. Even if the public library was not part of the agenda, librarians were there to represent it by their presence. Other civic meetings were also attended so that the men and women who made budget and policy decisions for the library made them with librarians conspicuously present.

Citizen Support of the Budget

The public librarian got in touch with as many interested library users in the community as possible so as to have them present for the preliminary hearings on the general budget, which included the library budget. Nonlibrarians stood up to speak in favor of increased library funds and to decry the unfortunate conditions of the library and its deterioration over the years.

Friends of the Library

Librarians worked to rejuvenate the Friends of the Library group, since its members were respected residents of the community. Besides this, the Friends had $30,000 in their treasury and needed some direction.

New Books in the Newspaper

Every week the library had published in both newspapers a list of its new books. The list, briefly annotated, sometimes emphasized the new mysteries, sometimes the best-sellers. A new book on Alaska was always given special attention.

Announcements of Library Meetings

Times, places, and dates of all meetings of the local chapter of the Alaska Library Association were always published beforehand in the newspaper. The topic of discussion was also announced, since it inevitably dealt with the improvement of the public library. The public was invited to attend these meetings.

In the meantime other means were used to publicize the public library, including mailing registration cards to homes, developing and publicizing a mail-back service for returning library books, and presenting to civic and neighborhood groups explanations of the statewide regional library plan, which would vitally affect the service and funds available to the Fairbanks public library.

Result: Extraordinary Notice

Results of these efforts of a small group of librarians brought extraordinary notice to the plight of the public library, exactly what local chapter members intended and hoped. Patrons said, "I heard the review on the radio and wondered if I could reserve the book." Others came into the library for the first time, looked around, and said, "Yes, you do need a new building."

This gratifying response confirmed the fact that a blanket approach was far more effective than isolated attempts at publicity. A new library building has usually been a project that takes years to accomplish from the time librarians initiate the momentum. In Fairbanks the tactic of making known the services of the public library, and thereby bringing more people into the building to see for themselves its cramped, unpleasant conditions, worked. Fairbanks has a new library.

PART THREE

18   Public Library Ideas

Of all types of libraries, a public library serves the broadest clientele. Public-library users include the entire range of age and intellectual levels. However, service only to those who venture up the steps and into the chambers is not enough. Aggressive development of promotional projects that attract as many people as possible to a community library is necessary. Such projects are expressions of progress and justification of the existence of the library itself. Public librarians must not take for granted, because jobs have always been available in the past, that they will inevitably have jobs in the future.

Public libraries around the country that hum with activity and are used by the young and old, the stay-ins and drop-outs, are the libraries that look to the future by promoting the present. They are the ones that not only bloom with neighborhood energy but also prosper with increased budgets.

To meet the needs of current users of public libraries and to attract nonusers, librarians must be prepared to experiment with promotional ideas of all types. Some will fail, some succeed. Some are more difficult than others, but all of them will help place a perspective on the importance of public relations for the area you service.

Here are some suggestions:

1) *Sponsor a photographic contest.* Get in touch with local photo-supply shops for advice and support. One of the stores may donate prizes, and probably one of the judges. A newspaper editor and a teacher of photography could be the other judges. Divide the contest into juvenile, young adult, and adult sections. Display the top twenty or thirty photographs (or however many you choose) in the library before the final decisions. When the judges pick the first three winners of each group, publish their photos in the newspaper and exhibit them further in the library. Stretch the publicity

for the library over a month with posters in the photo shops and announcements in the newspapers. Distribute lists of the best books on photography in the library. Nearly everyone has a camera these days. Nearly everyone should be interested in the library as well. Join the two in such a contest.

2) *Invite a nearby university professor to conduct a short series of courses or lectures on the Great Books of the Western World.* The series could be a primer for the professor's own course at the university. He or she might find that a different type of person may be attracted to the series from your library, thereby bringing fresh viewpoints into the classroom. On the other hand, many members of your community may still consider the public library a storehouse of only mysteries and science fiction. Here's your chance to show them that your library is also concerned with promoting interest in the great works of literature and social commentary. The series may not attract as many people as a fitness group, but it would diversify your overall program and fulfill the needs of an important community minority.

3) *Have an area in your children's room set aside for artwork drawn by the children themselves.* Either formally or informally, have children draw their own version of illustrations inspired by books they have read in the library. A wall of children's drawings with their names, ages, home addresses, and schools is always attractive both to other children and to their parents. Photograph an especially fine drawing and publish it in a newspaper as a sample of what is being done in the children's section. Such a feature in the library could be continued indefinitely. Prizes might be awarded for the best drawings, or they might be used in displays in the adult area.

4) *Hold a lecture series on social security benefits.* Federal laws in this area change, and members of the older generation with little income often miss new opportunities simply because they do not have the chance to learn about these changes. Social security benefits now include many programs devoted to individuals of all ages. Many people are not aware of this and would be surprised to learn how they may be advantageously affected by a program that was once thought of as being entirely geared to people over sixty-five. People are interested in how to raise their income. Your library can help them.

5) *Draft a bibliography on how best to invest money.* Include books and magazine articles; refer to your pamphlet file if you have such material in it. Be sure that you annotate the list with at least one or two lines of information, as a good library should. Then distribute these bibliographies at banks and savings-and-loan companies around town or pass them out at your lecture series on social security benefits.

6) *Show films and videos of general interest.* Perhaps you'll find that the popularity of such a free program might be carried over from the summer months into the winter. A standard year-long program of movies on a weekly or monthly basis could attract widespread family interest. You might have two types run on two different days. One would appeal to a general audience, the second to more specialized interests. A large number of non-commercial movies are being made each year. Include selection of everything from travelogues of exotic islands of the world to analyses of the light spectrum, to the space program, to mountain climbing. Show some of the better Hollywood and foreign films of old. One staff member could coordinate the entire program. Print and distribute time-and-place schedules. The newspaper may print them on a regular basis. The popularity of movies helps popularize your library.

7) *Take a poll among readers of what they consider the best book they ever read.* Then publish the list as one from local users of the library rather than the "best books" often chosen by professional critics and librarians. The survey might enlighten you about local priorities. Even more, it would give readers an idea of the tastes of their neighbors. People like to read what friends are reading. This type of list provides this friendship. Place a simple form at the chargeout desk. One title from each reader who wished to participate is enough. Later, post the results at the library entrance and in the newspaper. If one particular title has an overwhelming response, this could be used as an interesting item for radio and television newscasts. A lot of mileage may be had with little effort.

8) *Enter all parades.* Nearly every community has at one time or another during the year some sort of parade or civic celebration. The public library should be represented at every one. Let the public know that they have a free municipal library and that their library is front and center along with

other civic agencies. Libraries with bookmobiles can easily decorate their wagons of reading with signs and ribbons appropriate to the celebration theme. Some of the library workers might enjoy walking in the appropriate theme costume and passing out bookmarks or library registration blanks to the people at curbside. Even if no more is possible than riding in an open car with a sign on the door, be sure to enter. It's effortless publicity.

9) *Sponsor a music group.* So much of the population is under twenty-five years of age that public librarians must make special efforts to attract this age group to the library. Your town may have many small amateur music groups that would appreciate an opportunity for a free stage. A concert of two or three local groups on a Saturday night, either inside the library or on the grounds, could attract an age group that might otherwise assume a library has nothing relevant to offer. A local concert at the public library would also undoubtedly make the local news media.

10) *Conduct a book fair.* You might work with a local bookstore and specialize in promoting children's books or local history or a combination of mysteries and science fiction. Set up tables on the front lawn or porch. If the weather is inclement, set aside an area inside the library. Have cookies and punch or coffee available. Paint big signs with red letters and run streamers from tree to tree, window to window, or bookshelf to bookshelf. Generate a festive atmosphere. Make the world of books what it is—enjoyable.

11) *Offer the library building or grounds for speeches of visiting dignitaries or prominent authors.* Check with city hall personnel periodically to see if a visit by political leaders or big-business officials is planned in the near future. Suggest the library as an ideal central, nonpartisan location for speeches and welcoming committees. Also, try to place your library on the list of city sights that visitors should see, including a quick but pleasant tour of your most prized possessions. This pride in your library sparks similar pride and interest on the part of other city officials and community residents. The association of prominent personages with your library can only upgrade your image of importance to the people of your town.

12) *Set up a library booth downtown every Saturday.* A small,

colorful painted cubicle on the corner of the central shopping area is a reminder to harried shoppers that the library offers them a healthy breather in their lives. You must secure permission from the city for such a booth but should be able to do so without too much trouble. Station an attractive assistant inside to issue library cards to passersby and hand out book lists. The assistant might also take requests for books back to the library and then have them ready for pickup at the circulation desk when the patron goes to the library in the next two or three days.

13) *Drive the bookmobile to factories.* Some librarians use their bookmobiles only for schools and only during certain hours of the day. As a result, the bookmobile often stands idle and is not used to full potential. Experiment with your bookmobile during these unused times by peddling books to factory workers. Find out when coffee breaks are scheduled during mornings and afternoons at nearby factories or offices and meet this schedule at a few stops. Commercial lunch wagons do it all the time. A book wagon could offer appropriate reading refreshment to the workers at the same time. Make bookmobile stops at shopping malls and supermarkets along the way. An expensive machine like a bookmobile cannot afford to be sitting idle in the parking lot.

14) *Insert library information in other cultural program material.* Place specialized book lists and library schedules and circulation procedures in art-show guides, museum brochures, stage-production notes, and program publications handed out at cultural presentations. With a professional-looking insert, you shouldn't have much difficulty in convincing the management of your plan. A pleasing one-pager is sufficient. Your audience is captive and appropriate besides. The library insert provides an attractive addition not usually found in such programs and represents the library at quality events.

15) *Stage open houses periodically to introduce newcomers to your library.* An exceptional exhibit deserves more than a casual glance by someone walking through the building. So announce a library open house in the newspaper, decorate a table with cookies and coffee, invite some appropriate special guests, and present a short explanation of the exhibit. Open houses and an informal, friendly atmosphere create an oppor-

tunity for you and your staff to meet members of your community and to establish a better rapport with them and their needs.

16) *Conduct a workshop on how to use the public library.* Such a workshop may be valuable to many casual visitors to your library. The average layperson knows little about good library use. A workshop in the morning or afternoon (or the evening to catch the day workers) might be met with enthusiasm. Cover the basics of what is on a catalog card, how the Dewey Decimal or Library of Congress classification systems are arranged, the most-used reference books. Have an ample supply of printed information distributed at the workshop for the participants to take home with them. By the initial response you can decide whether more one-day workshops would be valuable or whether you might move toward more detailed instruction.

17) *Distribute a list of home reference materials that may be purchased inexpensively.* Include in the list books available at your library so that patrons may check to see what they contain. Parents constantly ask public librarians their judgment of the best encyclopedia to purchase for their school children at home. When they discover the cost of encyclopedias their purchase is usually postponed and nothing takes its place. A home reference collection suggested by your library is a welcome replacement. The following list won't take the place of an encyclopedia, but it helps:

World Almanac
Columbia-Viking Desk Encyclopedia
Random House Dictionary of the English Language, College
    Edition
(Dictionary of place names in your state)
Bartlett's Familiar Quotations
Guinness Book of World Records
Rand McNally World Atlas

Part of the cost may be spent for reference books in favorite subject areas. Here are only a few possibilities:

Benet's Reader Encyclopedia (for literary areas)
Encyclopedia of World History (for history)
Webster's New Dictionary of Synonyms (for writing)
Complete Guide to Everyday Law (for law)

18) *Begin a campaign to achieve 100-percent library registration of people or households in your community.* At the same time construct a tall "thermometer" of progress and station it on your front lawn or beside the entrance to the building. Indicate by red paint up the center of the thermometer the current registration percentage. Indicate on one side the number of people or households in your community (which you may easily secure at City Hall). Then keep a running tabulation of your actual number of registrants and of the number of possibilities. This giant thermometer gives you both an excuse to solicit new names and a publicity gimmick to exploit in the local newspaper.

19) *Have a remote radio broadcast periodically from your library.* Interview shows are the life-blood of many radio stations around the country. Perhaps no one at your nearest station ever suggested a show from the public library, where the array of fascinating people is virtually endless. Scholars, drop-outs, members of women's-liberation groups, seers, writers, researchers: the entire gamut of daily library users whom you may take for granted may be a discovery for program managers. The response could be so successful that the radio station will wish to make a regular feature of remote broadcasts from your library.

20) *Supply the local newspaper with a question-and-answer quiz.* Your reference librarian should be able to come up with five easy questions and answers a day. If not, then perhaps a ten-question quiz for the Sunday edition would work. A quiz is one of those simple feature items in a newspaper that many people try their heads with daily. Be sure that the name of your library is assigned to the quiz, as a place to find answers to these and other more personal questions, a place to keep in mind.

19   School Library Ideas

A school library is designed primarily to support the general curriculum of a school and to provide recreational reading as an enhancement of this curriculum. Materials in a school library must be kept relevant and up-to-date with an evolving instructional program. This way the library is integrated effectively into an overall education goal, that is, to activate each child's individual potential with the latest and fullest scope of materials possible.

More than any other type of library, with the possible exception of some special libraries, the school library has taken the lead in moving toward extensive use of other media as well as print materials. The trend toward instructional-materials centers at elementary, junior high school, and secondary levels is indicative of the vital role a school library plays in education. No longer is a library stocked only with books and pamphlets. Now, videotapes, slides, maps, audiotapes, individualized listening stations, charts, pictures, multimedia kits, television, computers, periodicals, microfilm, microfiche, and other materials are part and parcel of the modern instructional materials center, once known as a library.

The challenge to utilize the entire range of a school library is no small one. All these pieces of equipment and materials are of little focused use unless they are incorporated into the classroom curricula. School librarians must exert their professionalism by aggressively promoting their library. Otherwise, their programs will be directed by the relatively uninformed suggestions of others. Use of a school library does not depend nearly so much on the children in the classroom as it does on the teacher and other adults involved in the education of the young.

A combination, therefore, of making a school library attractive to students and adults alike is paramount. Here are some suggestions:

1) *Ask teachers what units they may be preparing for the near future.* If a unit on space exploration is planned, suggest to the teacher that you can prepare a short lesson in the library or in the classroom on reference books and supplementary material on space that may be helpful and interesting to students. Emphasize materials that have been published or acquired recently. Mention a new film or video relevant to the unit and suggest showing it in the library along with a short lesson on materials on the shelves that may be used immediately after and in conjunction with the movie. Keep yourself informed of the units teachers plan and then try to meet those units with materials they might find useful. Make good teachers of them and they'll come back for more.

2) *Prepare a videotape on the better use of the school library.* Many school districts are now producing their own tapes for instructional television programs as complements to the tapes they receive from the national network. Make certain the library is represented in your local series. A one-shot lesson is better than none. A series on: 1) generating enthusiasm and introducing the library in general; 2) the organization of the library; 3) reference and other nonfiction materials; 4) fiction, and a brief review, would provide the opportunity to particularize the television lesson to your own school district. The first production demands work, but the tape may be used many times after this and reap long-lasting benefits.

3) *Develop a story hour.* Some school librarians schedule a regular time during the school day to tell stories with books. Other possibilities include a story hour right after the last bell rings or on Saturday afternoon. Often the school library is unused during summer months. If a local public library has no summer program, the school library could be used for such story activities. This opening of the library would be a solid preparation for the regular session, when students return to classes. Try to set aside a certain area in the library for the story hours. A rug to sit on, a few chairs, and a cozy corner make the storytelling a little more appealing.

4) *Give book talks periodically.* Select some of the finer books relevant to both the class unit and the types of children in the class. Then arrange with the teachers for you to take a few minutes to generate interest in new titles, as well as the

classics that need to be introduced to new students each year. Be sure to emphasize to students that other good books are available if the ones you present are checked out, and that you will be more than pleased to help anyone find a book that appeals.

5) *Organize a library club.* Such a club not only develops better awareness of library use among its members but also establishes a relationship with the rest of the students by opening the library administration to young people. Library club members may give tours to younger students and parents during open houses, help with such daily work as keeping circulation records and shelving, and set up exhibits and displays. With some help they may also publish their own newsletter and suggest books for other students to read. They could also help you design library-aid materials, such as bookmarks and posters.

6) *Demonstrate the use of audiovisual equipment.* The school librarian in an instructional materials center must be familiar with the slide projectors, video cassettes, film projectors, record-tapes, film-loop machines, microfilm readers, and equipment needed to make audiovisual materials usable. The direction toward more individualized instruction, however, warrants student familiarity with these machines as well. Teachers, who in most states must take audiovisual courses for certification, also need refreshers on how to fix machines. Your demonstrations of these to a few students and teachers at a time may be extremely valuable and lead to more use of your expensive multimedia materials.

7) *Present a slide program to the school board.* A short, information-packed presentation that shows the goals of your library program in action may keep school-board members aware of library activities and predispose them to back your policies and proposals in the future. Take 35mm color slides of students and teachers using your materials. Have plenty of action in the pictures, no obvious poses. Prepare a short script with solid information and statistics. Then request a time slot in one of the board meetings for the presentation of ten minutes or less, no more. Stick to this ten minutes. Convince the board members with concrete evidence, not wishes and myths, that the library program they support is an active one

and contributes substantially to the overall effectiveness of the schools they govern.

8) *Publish a newsletter for teachers and administrators.* The newsletter could have the effect of informing the school-board members, superintendent, principals, and classroom teachers of new material available while at the same time keeping the library program up front in public view. Working for the students is your primary responsibility. All the good programs you develop or hope to develop do little good, however, unless they have the support of the administrators. One effective way to develop this support is to keep the administrators informed of your activities. Let them know once a month, in a photocopied one-sheet newsletter, of unusual displays, special programs at certain schools, library-staff participation in other school activities, how much new sets of materials are being used, about any increases in the use of the library as a result of certain innovations, and about other activities.

9) *Develop an "Our Library Is . . . " display for the next PTA meeting.* Have some of the students from all grade levels write short lines about what they think a library is and why it is important. Either have the students themselves print the statement on large paper or copy them on a large-type typewriter. Then paste the words on a piece of cloth-covered backing and set up a display table. Statements in the students' own words (such as "Without libraries the whole world would be in a mess up") give parents and teachers alike not only a few smiles and chuckles but an indication that children do consider their library important.

10) *Alternate grades for library exhibits.* Set aside one particular display area to be used solely by the students themselves. Give each grade level or class, depending on the size of the school, a turn in the preparation and execution of a library display. Within bounds of taste, let the students display exactly what they wish. Let them take the initiative in producing ideas. Guide them perhaps in the use of materials but allow them complete freedom in the use of their show-case. Indicate which grade prepared the current display and give credit to the individuals involved. In a short time competition should develop to see which grade can come up

with the best display. Such competition brings both notice and students to the library.

11) *Paint a long mural on incidents or information on one subject culled from various books.* You might suggest this as a project to one of the classroom teachers or you might have your library club members work on it. A fifteen- or twenty-foot piece of butcher paper and some watercolor paints are all the materials needed. Space travel, the history of your state, the water cycle, the Civil War—any number of subjects may be the focus. Students could illustrate the mural with scenes they have read in books on whatever subject they choose. The title, author, and call number could be painted next to the scene taken from the book. Afterward, hang the mural on a wall in the library or place it in the hall somewhere in public sight.

12) *Work toward flexible scheduling.* The trend toward a closer arrangement of student time and following more closely the student's immediate inclination of interest is appropriate to the use of a library also. The need to go to the library to research a subject the moment the need arises should not be blocked. Arrange with classroom teachers and principals to allow students to go to the library when students themselves are ready, not merely when you are ready. Flexible scheduling brings the library into the forefront of the student's learning process, a process that cannot be departmentalized into time slots or artificially created.

13) *Conduct tours of the library for new teachers.* Make a concerted effort to have a spot in the new-teacher orientation program for a brief in-person explanation of your library facilities and materials. No matter how brief, such a tour establishes the library as a central organ of the school program, familiarizes new teachers with the capability of the library, and allows you the opportunity to invite them to use your services so that they may become better teachers and in turn create better students.

14) *Prepare a photo spread for the local newspaper.* Let the community at large know that the library program is integral to the overall education of its children. Some school districts have their own public relations personnel; they should be notified to execute such a picture page. If not, then you may either get in touch with the editor of the paper and ask him to

send one of his photographers or you will have to track down a photographer (such as yourself) to take the photos. Don't forget you have an edge. Newspaper editors know that most people like to see photos of children. Make sure your pictures are full of action, that they tell a story, and that they have a professional quality equal to your professional interest in the library.

15) *Develop student library skills in multimedia.* Offer to teachers and principals to organize some small workshop sessions in which you would provide practice for students to research a subject in the wide variety of formats available in the library. With a teacher, prepare a plan to expose students to a broad range of information on, for example, personal hygiene. List the films, videos, books, pamphlets, listening-station material, pictures, charts, and other media available on this one subject. Concentrate on generating awareness in students that research information is available in many other forms than books and that using a variety of media in your library makes research projects more fun.

16) *Send classroom ideas to teachers.* At times some teachers become annoyed when outsiders seem to intrude into their classroom domains. However, most competent, enthusiastic teachers welcome new ways to present old ideas. Photocopy any unusual article, or photograph of a striking bulletin board, or list of effective learning steps in presenting mathematical concepts, and send them to appropriate teachers. Read nonprofessional magazines also, because many contain informative articles on education. Give a teacher the feeling that you are in the library to serve them, that they are really not alone in the classroom, and demonstrate your interest in how well they teach by periodically passing along tricks of the trade from other competent, enthusiastic teachers in the country.

17) *Experiment with paperbacks.* The amazing spread of paperbound books is symptomatic of their appeal to readers of all ages. Paperbacks may be displayed in a separate paperbound section, on a spin-rack as in drugstores, or incorporated within the main section of the book shelves. Suggest to teachers that students have their own paperbound dictionaries at their desks. The cost is minimal for the long-range benefits such a handy personal dictionary may

bring. Every classroom should also have a couple of paper-bound almanacs. Many suitable fiction books for school children are published in paperback and may be processed informally for library use. The affinity young people have for paperbound books outside the school building should be put to advantage inside the library.

18) *Have students prepare their own bibliographies.* Announce that the library is seeking students to make a list of the five best books they have ever read. With short annotations, the students can write the reasons that they enjoyed the books. Publish the list in some form and then distribute it in their classrooms. Students sometimes are more likely to read a book suggested by their peers than by a teacher or librarian. Student-produced bibliographies give them this suggestion. They also give students skills in preparing bibliographies in proper form and a concentrated interest in what a library has provided them.

19) *Show films or videos after school in your library.* Select movies that have been recently shown in classrooms by teachers as part of certain lessons. This will not detract from your potential audience, since children like to see movies a second or third time. In addition, the repeat showings help reinforce the learning process. You could select movies from each class level and show them on certain days of the week so that a pattern results: movies for lower grades on Monday, middle grades on Wednesday, upper grades on Friday. Keep the atmosphere relaxed and informal. Make the library a center of activity and as important as the playground.

20) *Attend all school meetings and functions.* Through you the library should be represented at PTA meetings, school-board meetings, principal meetings, faculty meetings, rallies, parties, assemblies, sports events, the entire range of school activities. The library gains a certain stature through librarians who are attentive to the current needs of the school program and who exhibit a professional interest in how their own program relates to the overall educational goals. Volunteer for committee work—and produce. Make your opinions and aims for the school library known. Public exposure and the acquaintances you make by attendance at many school-related functions establish the image of your library as a dynamic and aggressive center of service.

20 College and University Library Ideas

Most first-year undergraduates in college are as nervous as the northern lights. They don't know where to go and they don't know whom to ask. Suddenly they're under an avalanche of assignments. From the first class onward their world becomes more mysterious by the day: they are being intellectually born.

Without some help they either flounder through the harried halls of learning on the principle of the survival of the fittest, or become needlessly discouraged and serve their four-year term without the excitement and skill of being intellectually assured.

Librarians enjoy a great opportunity to win these nervous newborns to their side. And just as undergraduates have many unvoiced needs, so do the most advanced researchers in dark corners of the campus. Many individuals at all levels on a college or university campus don't really know what is in their library, let alone challenge its potential or resources.

A college or university library is designed to support the curriculum of an institution. This curriculum is usually broad-based and serves a highly varied clientele. Universities normally include the four levels of undergraduate instruction, graduate levels from masters to doctoral degrees, postgraduate courses, special institutes, and laboratory research. Anyone in any of these programs is likely to miss much pertinent material, because so much is published in and around the fields that it is impossible for any individual to keep abreast of it.

Librarians should keep in mind that they, too, are involved in a program and not merely a place. Extending their program of services to the full range of needs of a campus should be priority number one. The library as a program is always more important than the library as a place.

Part of your program is to keep everyone, from undergraduate to researcher, library conscious and informed of your resources and services. Here are some suggested ways to do it:

1) *Write a library column for the campus newspaper.* Make it lively, jumpy, and refreshing. Avoid the standard book-review column. Call it "Bookie" or "Letterhead" or "Library-land." Laugh it off a little. Write about some of the great books to browse through, like the *Guinness Book of World Records.* Write as personally as you can. The undergraduates will be your major audience. Get to know their problems and then write about how the library may help them. Write about the latest scientific facts on drugs, what the great philosophers said about cheating, what the military budget is compared to that of the Department of Education, how conservation affects their lives. A good column keeps up with today. Have the column appear in the paper as regularly as possible. The fact that it's there is publicity. It's better publicity if it's read. This depends on how you write it.

2) *Develop one-page annotated bibliographies on current interests.* Produced on a regular schedule, the bibliographies could provide sources of background reading on the top issues of the day. If the Japanese make the headlines about opposing nuclear-energy development, a quick bibliography on the historical reasons would be a handy service. A box labeled "Have You Read These?" may be mounted at strategic spots on campus, such as in the commons or the gym or the bookstore, anywhere people move a lot together. Be sure the bibliography bears the name of the library and that it is dated and initialed. Be sure that all bibliographies, large or small, are annotated in some way. Librarians are in the business of bibliographies. Their products should be informative and authoritative.

3) *Send book jackets by intracampus mail to professors as an effective current-awareness tool.* They may also be used for exhibit and display background. Most libraries remove the jackets before processing books for the stacks. When the jackets are discarded, so, unfortunately, is a great deal of planning and expense by the publisher to attract readers to this particular book. Most jackets on books today jump with vitality. Librarians should make use of the modern typography, bright colors, and magnetic designs. Cut off the sides and

back of the jackets and send a batch of relevant front covers to professors. This little extra effort demonstrates to the faculty that librarians care that new acquisitions are known and read. The same service to graduate students and undergraduates would no doubt win a host of smiling loyalists.

4) *Bookmarks may be easily distributed from the circulation or information desks.* Bookmarks are an efficient way of keeping the simple word "library" before the public. At comparatively little cost, a commercial printer can design bookmarks with the name of your library, the hours you're open for service, and a one-line quote, something like "Beware the man of one book." On the reverse side it may be possible to print an abbreviated form of the circulation policies and procedures. The bookmarks can be automatically inserted in books at the circulation desk by the student clerks or left in piles near the charge-out area. Readers always need them.

5) *An exchange board located in the library may draw more people in.* People gravitate to bulletin boards, either to read messages out of pure curiosity or to hunt for bargains. Such a board in the lobby of the library is one more evidence that your library is a true information center where people may find what they need. So the board is messy. It's a people-getter, and this takes precedence. Reserve the right to clean the board once a month. The board also provides an excellent opportunity to sneak in library news of one sort or another.

6) *Send a selected list of new acquisitions to appropriate departments on campus.* Many librarians expect professors to take the initiative in learning what new materials the library has received. Most professors don't have the time or simply don't care. Some libraries send receipts from order slips to the professors who request certain titles. This is a good service to let individual professors know when the books they ordered have arrived. It might be more effective to send a list of pertinent new acquisitions once every three or four weeks to the entire department. A nicely typed list of the newest sociology books or oceanography books or whatever could be posted at the department bulletin board. Such a list should be profitable to both faculty and librarians.

7) *Develop a library-related radio program for the campus station.* Most program managers would be speechless if you approached them about such an idea. They always need

series. The program could go in virtually any direction you wished and probably could be of any time length. A five-minute program might delineate new material in the library or talk about quick research in various subject fields. The library could sponsor the reading of modern short stories (selected from the stacks, of course). A longer program might focus on campus professors and how they use library facilities to develop their subject fields. A thirty-minute program could use a magazine format in which just about anything goes— interviews, readings, questions and answers, opinions, music, recorded plays, panel discussions on current topics. The important factor, besides having an interesting series, is that the library extend its voice beyond its own walls.

8) *A sign of the day is always eye-catching and habit-forming.* In some prominent place, perhaps next to a calendar, a blackboard or a large piece of paper could be displayed that would tell what significant person was born this day or what even took place. Each day the sign would change. The Gale *Literary Calendar,* for instance, gives the birthday of important writers throughout history. The sign on February 2 might read "James Joyce, born 1882." One or two of his more famous books might be listed below. *Chases' Calendar of Annual Events* is another easy source. Outlines of history according to year and day are other sources. Such a feature makes a library interesting, and also provokes conversation.

9) *A series of lectures or demonstrations explaining the rare-book collection would answer many questions.* Rare books have always had a mysterious aura about them. Such a series held among the rare books themselves would not only extend the meaning of a library to many but might also develop interest in a collection that is often much neglected. The series could either be conducted by the rare-book librarian or by library-using professors, who could explain books in their fields. Such fundamental questions as what makes a rare book rare, criteria for classifying rare books, how they are pre-served, the significance of the ingredients of paper in the mid-nineteenth century, old techniques of printing, how to use rare books, and how they are important to a university collection could be discussed and evoke interest.

10) *Memos to professors asking how you may help their classes might produce enthusiastic response.* A quick note to professors

might hit them at a time when they need fresh material on a particular aspect of their course but don't have time to collect it. Or they may invite you to present their classes with short talks on the best sources to track down references to an important but little-known person in history. Or they may ask you to draw up an outline for their undergraduates on how to prepare a bibliography. If you follow through, you've made a lasting friend. Of course, they may say, no, thank you, they haven't used the library since they received their doctorates. Either way, your initiative is one more step toward making the library a program instead of a place.

11) *Circulate a digest of the library's annual report around the various campus departments.* Annual reports have always been necessary evils in the library world. Nevertheless, with some bright-colored paper and some daring typography, a few light-hearted comments about the library's being the heart attack of the university, a one- or two-page summary of new services, significant acquisitions, and general statistics may keep the rest of the campus community, not merely administrators, in touch with librarians. After describing what the library offered during the past year, a few words from the chief librarian about future plans and hopes might ease the way to achieving these plans and hopes. Again, small efforts lead to big results.

12) *Tours of a library are a good introduction to its services and materials.* Small groups of twenty people or less are the best. Whatever size, the tours should give information that cannot be easily obtained any other way. Or why have the tour? Reasons for ordering certain obscure material, what exactly catalogers do during the day, current progress in microforms, why encyclopedias are replaced, how your library fits into the national scheme of information networks, and other behind-the-scenes information spark tours to life. The majority of people simply have no concept of the complexity of a library. A tour is a good opportunity to educate the layperson to this complexity. It's also a good opportunity to make library friends out of library strangers. And always be sure to give each member of the tour something to take away. It could be a one-sheet floor plan or a more involved description of circulation policies and procedures. Better yet, promote some of your favorite books along

the way and see who bites. If only one member of a tour checks out a book, you're a success.

13) *Sample reference questions are enjoyable to read.* A list of the "Best Reference Questions of the Week" could be printed in the campus paper or typed up and posted near the reference desk. Every information desk should keep a list of questions asked anyway. This is one way to use this list, and it may be effective. Students or faculty members may see that other unusual questions have been asked and answered. Maybe their questions about superconductivity will be answered, too. In addition, individuals would see that librarians are approachable, that they are there to help, that unusual questions are really not so unusual, that such questions should be asked, and that the library really is an answering service.

14) *Newsletters from your library offer the chance to initiate your own controlled publicity.* Newsletters, however, are only justified if they are read, and not merely looked at. Snappy format and snappy writing help steer you away from producing just another word sheet. Even at the university level the trick to readability is and always will be personal interest. Write a newsletter as if you're writing it to one person. Only one person is going to read it at a time anyway. Write informally and keep the content informative but easy to comprehend. Mention professors who come up with good ideas to improve library service. Concentrate on people in relation to their work rather than things in relation to the library. Write short sentences, write short paragraphs. People remember a library newsletter with zip and zest.

15) *A film series could be sponsored by the library.* A more traditional approach would be to pick films that have been produced from books, such as *The Pawnbroker* or *The Last Angry Man.* (Be sure you have the books in the stacks.) If facilities are available, the best place to show the films would be in the library itself. If the showing is elsewhere, remember to publicize clearly that the library is the sponsor, that the library is concerned and aware of contemporary outlets of culture. It might be feasible to have a short panel discussion by members of the drama and English departments about the relationship between the book and the film. Such a panel would have to be brief and to the point after a ninety-minute

College/University Library Ideas

223

film, but it could round off an exciting evening. The library would have provided it.

16) *A personal-library contest sponsored by the university library will generate outside interest if handled properly.* Many unusual collections surface for these contests. Such a contest may stimulate interest in the book world and open the eyes of people who don't think much about libraries at all. The publicity possibilities are obvious if participants enter their exotic personal libraries on great eighteenth-century pirates, extrasensory perception, witchcraft, pre-twentieth-century science fiction, Houdini, rogues, hobos, Will Rogers, black cowboys, phrenology, literary fakes, and other uncommon topics. Besides the fun, your acquisitions department may find some valuable leads.

17) *A lecture by a prominent national, regional, or local author sponsored or cosponsored by the library would be most appropriate.* The library, in a far more comprehensive way than the English department, should be concerned with literary matters and mass communications. An author speaking on the changing role of modern fiction, or how contemporary journalism has affected nonfiction, or the contribution of poets in a mass society, or other related subjects could draw good crowds and create interest. Such lectures underline the library as an integral part of the campus and its contribution to university culture beyond the mere charging in and out of materials.

18) *A good art exhibit on the main floor of the library brings in many nonlibrary users.* A controversial art exhibit brings in many more. Usually all you have to provide an artist is the space. The artist will do the rest. An exhibit may last from one day to one month, depending on the artist, the work, and the interest. The art doesn't have to be limited to campus artists. Painters and sculptors from a local community would probably jump at the chance to display their work on a university campus. Naturally, such an exhibit would lend itself to publicity in the local newspaper. Campus artists in the library would be reported in the university paper and bring notice. A constant change of events, exhibits, displays, and activities at the library makes for comment and attention. The library becomes an interesting place to go because it is alive and experimental.

19) *Forums at the library keep the focus of our part of the university where it should be—on the student.* A "Wednesday Hour" or something similar could be devoted to weekly meetings of interest. Either an area or seminar room of the library could be used for scheduled or unscheduled topics that concern students. Debates between Young Republicans and Young Democrats, question-and-answer periods with school administrators, student poetry readings, small panel discussions, guest speakers, all could be presented in a flexible format. Having such an informal outlet for student opinions in the library could win many friends for the future.

20) *An introductory reference course conducted by librarians and required of all students is probably the best way to open the mysteries of the library to as many students as possible.* Most universities have no such required course. Still, librarians should try to institute such a course in the curriculum. Not as satisfactory, but at least something, is working with members of the English department to allow a week or so for instruction in the fundamentals of the university library. A formal structure of library instruction makes official what librarians have always known—using a library effectively is the route to intellectual treasure.

APPENDIXES

Appendix A   Library Survey

This survey was developed and distributed by the Peterborough (N.H.) Town Library to ascertain the interests of its patrons and the services they use. The survey can be a guide for other libraries.

- Do you have a Public Library card? ___Y ___N

- When was the last time you visited the library?
  _____ within the past week
  _____ within the past 2 weeks
  _____ within the past month
  _____ within the past year
  _____ more than a year ago

- How do you find what you want in the library?
  _____ I browse
  _____ I ask a librarian
  _____ I use the catalog to locate items
  _____ My friends and I look them up together

- Which of our services do you use?
  _____ Reading area (newspapers/news magazines)
  _____ Magazines (back issues to check out)
  _____ In-person Reference
  _____ Telephone Reference
  _____ Movies (Nursing homes, etc.)
  _____ Movies for Kids
  _____ IRS forms
  _____ Library programs (Readings, etc.)
  _____ Friends of the Library programs
  _____ Atari computer
  _____ Story Time
  _____ Meeting Rooms
  _____ Children's Room (and the Children's Librarian)

227

_____ Photocopying
_____ Reserving books
_____ Microfilm
_____ Historical Room (Town histories, genealogies)
_____ Public bulletin board (Reading or listing things)
_____ Interlibrary loan

• Do you ever . . .
  . . . sit down and read our magazines and newspapers?
          _____Yes _____No
  . . . ask the advice of the librarians about book purchases *you*
  plan to make (encyclopedias, etc.)?
          _____Yes _____No
  . . . come to meet your family or friends here?
          _____Yes _____No

• What kinds of materials do you borrow from us?
  _____ Books from the Adult sections
  _____ Children's Books
  _____ Magazines
  _____ Videocassettes: _____Adult _____Junior
  _____ Pictures
  _____ Children's Book/Tapes (in bags)
  _____ Jigsaw Puzzles
  _____ N.H. State Publications
  _____ Vertical File materials
  _____ Typewriters
  _____ A-V (movie projector, slides, etc.)
  _____ Rock tapes (YA Tapes)
  _____ Audiocassettes
  _____ Large Print books
  _____ Records
  _____ Museum passes
  _____ Children's Pictures
  _____ Polaroid Camera

• When do you most often visit the library?
  Time of day: Day of the Week:
  _____ Morning (10–12)   _____ Sunday
  _____ Lunchtime (12–2)   _____ Monday
  _____ Afternoon (2–5)   _____ Tuesday
  _____ Evening (5–8)   _____ Wednesday
                                   _____ Thursday
                                   _____ Friday
                                   _____ Saturday

- Adults: Are you a resident of _____? ____Y ____N
  Child/Student: Do you live in the _____ School
    District? ____Y ____N

- Why do you read?
  _____ For relaxation
  _____ To keep myself informed
  _____ Habit
  _____ Homework
  _____ For business/research purposes
  _____ I read to my kids.
  _____ Other: _____
  _____
  _____

- What are your favorite subjects?
  _____ Best-seller fiction   _____ Biographies
  _____ Classic fiction   _____ Fine arts
  _____ Historical fiction   _____ Gardening
  _____ Mystery   _____ History
  _____ Romance   _____ Poetry
  _____ Science fiction   _____ Philosophy/Religion
  _____ Sports   _____ Science
  _____ Westerns   _____ Social sciences
  _____ Cookery   _____ Politics/Int. Relations
  _____ Essays   _____ Humor
  _____ Short stories   _____ Current events
  _____ Magazines   _____ Reading Rainbow books

- What kind of music do you like?
  _____ Classical   _____ Opera
  _____ Jazz   _____ Musicals
  _____ Country & Western   _____ Motion picture sndtrks.
  _____ Rock & Roll   _____ Popular/Vocalists
  _____ Other: _____

- Which do you prefer? ____Records ____Cassettes____CDs

- Do you use other libraries? ____Y ____N
  If yes, what libraries? _____
  _____

- What *do* you like about _____ Public Library?

  _____
  _____
  _____
  _____

- What *don't* you like about _____ Public Library?

  _____
  _____
  _____
  _____

  (Don't forget to include things like: Lights, ease of parking, convenience, availability, etc.)

- What do you wish we did/didn't have? _____
  _____
  _____
  _____

TELL US ABOUT YOURSELF (This section is optional.)

Age:
_____ 3–10 yrs.
_____ 10–15 yrs.
_____ 16–20 yrs.
_____ 21–30 yrs.
_____ 31–40 yrs.
_____ 41–50 yrs.
_____ 51–65 yrs.
_____ 65+ yrs.

Sex:
_____ Male
_____ Female

Marital Status:
_____ Single
_____ Married
_____ Divorced
_____ Widow/Widower
_____ (Other?)

Education (Adults):
_____ Didn't graduate from high sch
_____ High School grad.
_____ 2-yr. college or technical scho
_____ 4-yr. college
_____ Graduate study

Education (Children):
_____ Preschool/Kind.
_____ Elementary
_____ Middle/Jr. High
_____ High School

I consider myself to be: I watch:
_____ a light reader   _____ a little TV
_____ a moderate reader   _____ average amount of TV
_____ a heavy reader   _____ a lot of TV

(Note: there are no guide-
lines for light/moderate/
heavy reading or TV. This
is your own opinion.)

- Any other comments you would like to make:_____
  _____
  _____
  _____
  _____

Thank you for talking the time to fill out this form.

Appendix B   Notable Quotes from Quotable Notables

Never judge a book by its movie.—*J. W. Eagan*

Just the omission of Jane Austen's books alone would make a fairly good library out of a library that hadn't a book in it.—*Mark Twain*

Many contemporary authors drink more than they write.—*Gorki*

He who wields a pen is in a state of war.—*Voltaire*

A real book is not one that we read, but one that reads us.—*W. H. Auden*

Practically everybody in New York has half a mind to write a book—and does.—*Groucho Marx*

Already by 1900 I could boast I had written as many books as Moses.—*Winston Churchill*

My books are water; those of the great geniuses are wine—everybody drinks water.—*Mark Twain*

Read the best books first, or you may not have a chance to read them at all.—*Thoreau*

No man should ever publish a book until he has first read it to a woman.—*Van Wyck Brooks*

The chief objection to new books is that they prevent us from reading the old ones.—*Joubert*

It is with books as with men: a very small number play a very large part.—*Voltaire*

The real purpose of books is to trap the mind into doing its own thinking.—*Christopher Morley*

A book is a mirror; when an ass looks into it, don't expect an apostle to look out.—*G. C. Lichtenberg*

There is a great deal of difference between an eager man who wants to read a book and the tired man who wants a book to read.—*Chesterton*

The ordinary man would rather read the life of the cruelest pirate that ever lived than the wisest philosopher.—*Robert Lynd*

I have the reputation of having read all of Henry James, which would argue a misspent youth and middle age.—*James Thurber*

We read often with as much talent as we write.—*Emerson*

What is written without effort is read without pleasure.—*Samuel Johnson*

You moon-men, put Walden in your pocket.—*Lawrence Clark Powell*

Wear the old coat and buy the new book.—*Austin Phelps*

You think your pain and your heartbreak are unprecedented in the history of the world, but then you read. It was books that taught me that the things that tormented me most were the very things that connected me with all the people who were alive, or who had ever been alive.—*James Baldwin*

Beware the man of one book.—*Isaac D'Israeli*

Every abridgment of a good book is a stupid abridgment.—*Montaigne*

The virtue of books is to be readable.—*Emerson*

There is no such thing as a moral or immoral book. Books are well written, or badly written. That is all.—*Oscar Wilde*

A book that is shut is but a block.—*Thomas Fuller*

Books will speak plain, when counsellors blanch.—*Francis Bacon*

A big book is a great evil.—*Callimachus*

My library was dukedom large enough.—*Shakespeare*

Every library should try to be complete on something, if it were only the history of pinheads.—*O. W. Holmes*

It is not wide reading but useful reading that tends to excellence.—*Aristippus*

Let blockheads read what blockheads wrote.—*Lord Chesterfield*

I hate books; they teach us to talk about things we do not understand.—*Rousseau*

Each age must write its own books; or rather, each generation for the next succeeding. The books of an older period will not fit this.—*Emerson*

I never read a book before reviewing it. It prejudices me so!—*Sydney Smith*

If you want to learn about the mind of a nation, study its rental libraries.—*Wilhelm Hauff*

Books and libraries and the will to use them are among the most important tools our nation has to diffuse knowledge and to develop our powers of creative wisdom—*J. F. Kennedy*

A library, to modify the famous metaphor of Socrates, should be the delivery room for the birth of ideas—a place where history comes to life.—*Norman Cousins*

A library is not a luxury, but one of the necessities of life.—*H.W. Beecher*

Libraries are not made; they grow.—*W. J. Birrell*

A best-seller is the gilded tomb of a mediocre talent.—*Logan P. Smith*

The library has been created by actual necessities in modern civilization. It is now a necessary unit in the social fabric.—*Pierce Butler*

All the known nations, excepting only savage nations, are governed by books.—*Voltaire*

The pen is the tongue of the mind.—*Cervantes*

My early and invincible love of reading I would not exchange for the treasures of India.—*Gibbon*

It is not observed that librarians are wiser men than others.—*Emerson*

Appendix C   Useful Facts and Figures

The longest important novel ever published is *Remembrance of Things Past,* by Marcel Proust, with 1,307,000 words.

The first book printed in English (*The Recuyell of the Historyes of Troye*) was produced by William Caxton, about 1475, in Bruges.

The world's oldest printed book is *The Diamond Sutra,* produced in China in A.D. 868.

The art of writing was developed about 5,000 years ago by Sumerians.

The Bibliothèque Nationale of Paris is the oldest national library in the world.

John Harvard, in 1638, founded the first American college and first library in English-speaking America.

Benjamin Franklin founded the first subscription library in 1731.

In 1833 the Peterborough, N.H., library became the first free tax-supported public library in the world.

The classic Alexandrian Library once contained 700,000 rolls of manuscripts.

The American Library Association was founded in 1876, the Medical Library Association in 1898, the Special Libraries Association in 1909.

Andrew Carnegie gave construction money, beginning in 1882, for 2,507 libraries, including 1,689 in the United States, 660 in Great Britain and Ireland, and 125 in Canada.

The number of titles published in the first half of the twentieth century is estimated to be equal to the total published from the beginning of movable type in 1450 to 1900.

Louis Timothee, the first librarian in America to be paid a salary, earned three pounds sterling every four months in the library begun by Benjamin Franklin.

The first library convention in 1853 had eighty-two librarians in attendance.

In the fourth century A.D., Rome had twenty-eight public libraries.

Harvard University Library has 3,500 volumes printed before 1501.

Sir Thomas Bodley began the Bodleian Library at Oxford University in 1602 with 2,000 volumes.

Index

Image
    changeable, 21
    corporate, 21
Instructional materials centers, 210
Intellectual freedom, 70
Italy, 138

Japanese, 218
Japan Times, 32
Jessen's Daily, 195, 196
Johnson, Samuel, 233
Joubert, Joseph, 232
Joyce, James, 220

Keene (N.H.) Public Library, x, 41–51
    campaign, 48
    pledges, 48–49
    services, number of, 42
Kennedy, J. F., 234
Kenyon, Jane, 147
Kiwanis, 143
KUAC-FM (Alaska), 195
Ku Klux Klan, 77

The Last Angry Man, 222
The Last Temptation of Christ, 100
Lea, Sydney, 147
Legislative process, 173–175
Legislators, 167–170, 171, 172, 173, 196
Letters to TV networks, 184
Libraries
    number of, 34
    personnel, 223
    services, 145–146
Library Building Committee
    Wellfleet, Mass., 53, 55
Library Campaign Committee, 44
Library Club, 212, 214
Library column in newspapers, 140, 218
Library of Congress, 66
    classification, 208

About the Author

Steve Sherman received his B.A. in philosophy and M.A. in communication arts from Loyola University at Los Angeles, and an M.S. in Library Science from the University of California at Los Angeles (UCLA). While working as a reference librarian at the University of Alaska, he helped to develop projects involving newspapers, radio, film, video-tape, photo displays, and other programs promoting effective use of the library. His articles have appeared in *Wilson Library Bulletin, RQ, Film Quarterly,* and other professional journals. He is the New England correspondent for *Publishers Weekly* and the author and editor of 24 fiction and nonfiction books, including *A Scott Nearing Reader: The Good Life in Bad Times* (Scarecrow Press, 1989).